**Grammar, Usage,
and Mechanics Workbook**

Language
Network

McDougal Littell
A HOUGHTON MIFFLIN COMPANY
Evanston, Illinois • Boston • Dallas

ISBN 0-618-05262-3

12 13 14 15 16 17 18 19 20 – BHV – 06 05 04

Contents

Special Features v

❶ The Parts of Speech

  1) Nouns 1

  2) Personal Pronouns 4

  3) Other Kinds of Pronouns 7

  4) Verbs 10

  5) Adjectives 13

  6) Adverbs 16

  7) Prepositions 19

  8–9) Conjunctions and Interjections 22

❷ The Sentence and Its Parts

  1) Simple Subjects and Predicates 25

  2) Complete Subjects and Predicates 28

  3) Compound Sentence Parts 31

  4) Kinds of Sentences 34

  5) Subjects in Unusual Positions 37

  6) Subject Complements 40

  7) Objects of Verbs 43

  8) Sentence Diagramming 46

❸ Using Phrases

  1) Prepositional Phrases 49

  2) Appositives and Appositive Phrases 52

  3) Verbals: Participles 55

  4) Verbals: Gerunds 58

  5) Verbals: Infinitives 61

  6) Placement of Phrases 64

  7) Sentence Diagramming: Phrases 67

❹ Clauses and Sentence Structure

  1) Kinds of Clauses 70

  2) Adjective and Adverb Clauses 73

  3) Noun Clauses 76

  4) Sentence Structure 79

  5) Sentence Diagramming 82

❺ Writing Complete Sentences

  1) Sentence Fragments 85

  2) Run-On Sentences 88

6 Using Verbs

1) The Principal Parts of a Verb 91
2) Verb Tense 94
3) Progressive and Emphatic Forms 97
4) The Voice of a Verb 100
5) Shifts in Tense, Form, and Voice 103
6) The Mood of a Verb 106

7 Subject-Verb Agreement

1) Agreement in Number 109
2) Phrases Between Subject and Verb .112
3) Compound Subjects 115
4) Indefinite-Pronoun Subjects 118
5) Other Problem Subjects 121
6) Special Sentence Problems 124

8 Using Pronouns

1–2) Nominative and Objective Cases .127
3) The Possessive Case 130
4) Using Who and Whom 133
5) Pronoun-Antecedent Agreement 136
6) Indefinite Pronouns as Antecedents 139
7) Other Pronoun Problems 142
8) Pronoun Reference 145

9 Using Modifiers

1) Using Adjectives and Adverbs 148
2) Problems with Modifiers 151
3) Using Comparisons 154
4) Problems with Comparisons 157

10 Capitalization

1) People and Cultures 160
2) First Words and Titles 163
3) Places and Transportation 166
4) Organizations and Other Subjects 169

11 Punctuation

1) Periods and Other End Marks 172
2) Comma Uses 175
3) More Comma Uses 178
4) Semicolons and Colons 181
5) Dashes and Parentheses 184
6) Hyphens and Apostrophes 187
7) Quotation Marks 190
8) Ellipses and Italics 193

Special Features

The *Grammar, Usage, and Mechanics Workbook* contains a wealth of skill-building exercises.

Worksheets correspond to lessons in the Pupil's Edition.

Each page focuses on one topic or skill. A brief instructional summary on the **Reteaching** page is followed by reinforcement activities.

Key words and phrases are highlighted for greater clarity and ease of use.

When appropriate, example sentences demonstrate how to complete exercises.

Each lesson has different levels of worksheets. **Reteaching** introduces the skill; **More Practice** and **Application** extend the skill with advanced exercises.

Tabs make it easy to navigate the book.

Each page clearly refers to its corresponding part in the Pupil's Edition for easy reference.

Name _____ Date _____

Lesson 1

Prepositional Phrases

Reteaching

A **prepositional phrase** consists of a preposition, its object, and any modifiers of the object.

> Scientists observe stars <u>through a telescope</u>. (The preposition is *through*.)

An **adverb phrase** modifies a verb, an adjective, or another adverb.

> We see many stars <u>with the naked eye</u>. (The phrase modifies *see*, telling how.)

An **adjective phrase** modifies a noun or a pronoun.

> Light <u>from the stars</u> travels quickly. (The phrase modifies *light*, telling what kind.)

A. Identifying Prepositional Phrases

Underline the prepositional phrases in the following sentences.

> EXAMPLE Astronomers have made many discoveries <u>about the galaxy</u>.

1. Can anyone count the stars in the Milky Way?
2. The Milky Way looks beautiful on a clear night.
3. I enjoy stargazing from a nearby hilltop.
4. Clusters of stars form constellations.
5. Seven very bright stars surrounded by dust form the Seven Sisters.
6. Stars emit huge amounts of light.
7. Starlight passing through the atmosphere produces twinkling.
8. Stars change size, shape, and color in their life spans.
9. Different stars are fascinating to astronomers.
10. For centuries, people have looked into the heavens.

B. Identifying Words Modified by Prepositional Phrases

Underline the prepositional phrase in each of the following sentences once. Underline the word it modifies twice.

> EXAMPLE The quarterback <u>threw</u> the ball <u>into the end zone</u>.

1. Can you pronounce the name of the country?
2. The soprano sang one of my favorite songs.
3. In the cave an ancient artist had painted a hunting scene.
4. Along the path we planted pink and yellow tulips.
5. Can you see well in the dark?
6. The baseball flew over the fence.
7. Can you see that mountain in the distance?
8. The band played a song from a popular musical.
9. One of the hockey players was seriously injured.
10. During the storm all traffic stopped.

For use with Pupil's Edition pp. 66–68

GRAMMAR, USAGE, AND MECHANICS WORKBOOK **49**

CHAPTER 3

Copyright © McDougal Littell Inc.

Lesson 1 # Nouns

Reteaching

A **noun** is a word that names a person, place, thing, or idea.

Type of noun	Definition	Example
common noun	general name for a person, place, thing, or idea	state
proper noun	name of a particular person, place, thing, or idea	California
concrete noun	names an object that can be seen, heard, smelled, touched, or tasted	orange
abstract noun	names an idea, quality, or characteristic	trust
singular noun	one person, place, thing, or idea	tree
plural noun	more than one person, place, thing, or idea	trees
collective noun	name of a group	flock
compound noun	single noun formed from two or more words	grapefruit
possessive noun	noun that shows ownership or relationship	star's mansion

A. Finding Nouns

Underline every noun in each sentence.

1. Alaska is known for its cold weather and its abundance of natural resources.
2. While in Arizona, stop by the Grand Canyon for a view you will never forget.
3. If you like big trees, why not visit California, with its giant redwoods and sequoias?
4. Connecticut got its name from the Algonquin tribe; its name means "land on the long tidal river."
5. Explorer Ponce de León looked for the Fountain of Youth in the area that is now known as Florida.
6. Jesse James and his gang of desperate outlaws once roamed the state of Missouri.
7. New Orleans in Louisiana is one of the most exciting cities in the country.
8. Look for picturesque lighthouses in coastal states such as Maine.
9. Thomas Edison chose New Jersey as the best place for his laboratories.
10. See mammoth carvings of four presidents of the United States at Mount Rushmore in South Dakota.

B. Identifying Kinds of Nouns

Which word in parentheses describes the boldfaced noun? Underline the correct one.

1. An anthropologist wrote about the **beliefs** of the Samoans. (common, proper)
2. Pablo Picasso was a great **artist.** (concrete, abstract)
3. In ancient **Rome,** contests were held in the Colosseum. (common, proper)
4. Superman espoused "truth, **justice,** and the American way." (concrete, abstract)
5. The story of Odysseus's journey is a product of Homer's vivid **imagination.** (common, proper)
6. **Peter the Great** made Russia into a powerful nation. (common, proper)
7. The **planet** Mercury is closer than Mars to the sun. (concrete, abstract)
8. The British statesman Neville Chamberlain promised **"peace** in our time" just before the outbreak of World War II. (concrete, abstract)

Lesson 1

Finding Nouns

More Practice

A. Finding Nouns

Underline the noun or nouns described in parentheses after each sentence.

1. Mesa Verde National Park in Colorado gives visitors a glimpse of life in an ancient settlement of the Anasazis. (proper noun)

2. Visit Hawaii to see two active volcanoes, Mauna Loa and Kilauea. (common noun)

3. If you like winter sports, head for the beautiful ski slopes of Idaho. (plural noun)

4. While in the Midwest, visit Carl Sandburg's "city of the big shoulders"— Chicago. (possessive noun)

5. The Wright brothers tried out their first airplane near Kitty Hawk, North Carolina. (common noun)

6. Which state is proud of its tradition of tolerance? (singular noun)

7. A crowd of people moves through Grand Central Station in New York City, New York, daily. (collective noun)

8. English immigrants seeking religious freedom settled in Massachusetts in 1620. (abstract noun)

9. A racetrack in Indianapolis, Indiana, hosts the world-famous Indianapolis 500 each May. (compound noun)

B. Using Nouns

Replace each boldfaced noun in the list with the type of noun specified in parentheses. The new noun should reflect the same idea or subject as the boldfaced noun.

EXAMPLES **Abraham Lincoln** (common) *president*
food (compound) *pancake*

1. **New Jersey** (common) _____

2. **players** (collective) _____

3. **state** (proper) _____

4. **insect** (compound) _____

5. **recreation** (concrete) _____

6. **worker** (compound) _____

7. **geese** (collective) _____

8. **Detroit** (common) _____

9. **Brazil** (abstract) _____

10. **building** (proper) _____

For use with Pupil's Edition pp. 6–8

CHAPTER 1

Lesson 1

Using Nouns

Application

A. Using Nouns

Complete the paragraph by supplying nouns as indicated in parentheses. Write each word you would use on the blank line.

       While on the way to a reunion, Joseph's family drove through *(1. proper noun).* They stopped for a quick lunch near a *(2. common noun).* They were surprised to see a *(3. compound noun).* Without knowing it, they had spent hours at the stop. When they looked at the clock, they realized they would be late arriving at *(4. possessive proper noun)* house. They were looking forward to the *(5. concrete noun)* and to the *(6. abstract noun)* as well. They could hardly wait to see their whole *(7. collective noun)* again and to talk about old times with them.

1. _____

2. _____

3. _____

4. _____

5. _____

6. _____

7. _____

B. Writing with Different Kinds of Nouns

Rewrite each of the following sentences, replacing each boldfaced noun with the kind of noun indicated in parentheses. You may need to add, subtract, or change articles (*a, an, the*) in some sentences.

1. When I travel, I try to fit all my clothes in a light **trunk** (compound).

_____

2. Most seasoned travelers have **luggage** (abstract) and **credit cards** (abstract).

_____

3. The vacationer brought a new **attitude** (concrete) with her when she returned **home** (proper). (Add the word *to* to your new sentence.)

_____

4. Only about a **fraction** (compound) of the tour group on the bus spoke English.

_____

5. **Mr. Jimenez** (common) delivered his **speech** (plural) in both English and Spanish.

_____

Lesson 2 # Personal Pronouns   *Reteaching*

A **pronoun** is a word used in place of a noun or another pronoun. The word that a pronoun stands for is called its **antecedent.**

The <u>player</u> smiled as <u>he</u> waved to the crowd.
    ANTECEDENT   PRONOUN

Personal pronouns change form.

	Singular	Plural
First Person	I, me (my, mine)	we, us (our, ours)
Second Person	you (your, yours)	you (your, yours)
Third Person	he, him, she, her, it (his, her, hers, its)	they, them (their, theirs)

Possessive pronouns show ownership or relationship. The possessive pronouns are in parentheses in the chart above.

A. Finding Pronouns

Underline the pronouns in the following sentences.

EXAMPLE <u>She</u> is working on <u>her</u> backhand for the upcoming tennis match.

1. The batter holds his bat near the handle.
2. He never takes his eye off the ball as he swings for the fence.
3. The fans show their appreciation for the home run by standing and applauding.
4. The local team never wins the championship, but they are our team and we support them anyway.
5. If you could choose your favorite sport, what would it be?
6. If I knew its rules better, I would probably choose soccer.

B. Finding Pronouns and Antecedents

Underline all the pronouns in the following sentences. Underline their antecedents twice.

EXAMPLE The <u>squirrels</u> hid <u>their</u> food supply for winter in the hollow tree.

1. When dinosaurs walked the earth, they were impressive indeed.
2. Experts on dinosaurs say that they were the largest land animals ever.
3. Scientists gained much of their knowledge about dinosaurs during the 1800s.
4. In 1822, Mary Ann Mantell found a large dinosaur tooth and showed it to her husband, a fossil collector.
5. Other searchers found more dinosaur remains, and they pooled their knowledge.
6. Soon scientists were using the term *dinosaur* every time they referred to the huge lizard-like animals.
7. Imagine the excitement a scientist would feel when he or she found dinosaur bones!
8. The quest might keep a paleontologist interested throughout his or her whole life.

For use with Pupil's Edition pp. 9–10

Lesson 2

Personal Pronouns   *More Practice*

A. Finding Pronouns and Antecedents

Underline each personal or possessive pronoun once and its antecedent twice.

EXAMPLE The <u>player</u> tipped <u>his</u> cap while walking toward the dugout.

1. The ref asked the players to watch as he tossed the coin.
2. As soon as the game began, the fans began the chant they have made famous.
3. The vendor sent a snack down the row, and then he waited for the money.
4. When the wave reached her section, Lorna stood up and raised her arms.
5. The players listened to their coach when time was called.
6. The coach explained the play and emphasized its importance by raising his voice.
7. When the cheerleaders made a human pyramid, the crowd shouted its approval.
8. The head cheerleader received applause when she did a series of cartwheels.
9. As the fans made their way out of the stadium, they celebrated the win.
10. Football deserves its reputation as one of America's favorite sports.

B. Using Pronouns

Complete each sentence with an appropriate personal pronoun. Write it on the line.

EXAMPLE Maura knows what _____*she*_____ will order for lunch.

1. The principal makes _____ announcements over the public address system every day during homeroom.

2. All bus riders should pick up _____ passes at the office by 3:00 P.M.

3. When the clouds moved in, the day lost _____ appeal for me.

4. When we go for an all-day hike, we always take along _____ lunches.

5. When my aunt greets me, she always gives _____ a big hug.

6. I can't believe I forgot _____ homework today!

7. If you want to compete in this show, you and _____ dog should get into line.

8. If _____ memory serves me correctly, you prefer chocolate cake.

9. When band practice runs late, Sharon's mother usually drives _____ home.

10. I admire ants because _____ are so industrious.

Lesson 2

Personal Pronouns

Application

Write sentences following the directions for each item. Underline the required pronouns in your sentences.

1. Use a personal pronoun in the third-person singular as the subject of a sentence.

_____

2. Use a personal pronoun in the first-person plural as the subject of a sentence.

_____

3. Use a possessive pronoun in the second-person plural anywhere in the sentence.

_____

4. Use a possessive pronoun in the first-person singular anywhere in the sentence.

_____

5. Use a possessive pronoun in the third-person plural anywhere in the sentence.

_____

B. Writing with Pronouns

Write a short paragraph about a typical day in your life. Use a variety of personal pronouns. Underline each pronoun once and draw an arrow from it to its antecedent.

_____

_____

_____

_____

_____

_____

_____

_____

_____

_____

_____

_____

For use with Pupil's Edition pp. 9–10

Lesson 3 **Other Kinds of Pronouns**   *Reteaching*

Some kinds of pronouns perform special functions in sentences.

Type of pronoun	Function	Example
reflexive	represents the subject of its sentence or clause	myself
intensive	emphasizes a noun or pronoun in the same sentence	herself
demonstrative	points out specific persons, places, things, or ideas	that, those
indefinite	refers to unidentified persons, places, things, or ideas	each, most
interrogative	introduces a question	who, what
relative	introduces a noun clause or adjective clause	who, that

Finding Pronouns

Underline all the pronouns in the following sentences.

1. One really exciting activity is exploration.
2. Some famous explorers are the greatest heroes.
3. However, there are those who are not as well known.
4. For example, who was Helen Thayer? What did she do?
5. In 1988, Helen Thayer, who was 50 years old at the time, decided to travel to the magnetic North Pole.
6. She was determined to reach the Pole by herself; that was the major goal.
7. Helen journeyed to the North Pole with only a dog that was named Charlie.
8. Charlie's job was to protect Helen from all of the polar bears in the area.
9. This was a job that Charlie did well; although they were confronted by seven polar bears, one at a time, Helen completed the trip in safety.
10. No one helped Helen on the expedition; she herself pulled the sled.
11. Helen Thayer became the first woman to travel solo to either of the world's poles.
12. She wrote a book about the trip, which became a national bestseller.
13. On November 1, 1997, Helen began a new journey, which would be 200 miles long.
14. On November 12, which was her birthday, she lit a candle on a frozen cupcake and sang "Happy Birthday" to herself.
15. That was an exceptionally windy year, and the trip became a difficult one for her.
16. On the 22nd day of the expedition, a strong gust of wind caught the sled; the sled itself became a missile and slammed into Helen's left leg and hip.
17. She struggled to set up the tent by herself.
18. She was forced to ask herself, "What should I do? Should I go on or go back?"
19. She reminded herself of the family members and friends who were left behind, and decided to return to base camp.
20. Helen accepted this as another one of life's experiences.
21. She didn't blame herself for suffering a minor setback and soon set to work preparing herself for a new adventure.
22. Helen Thayer is one of many women who display the exploring spirit.

CHAPTER 1

Lesson 3

Other Kinds of Pronouns

More Practice

A. Identifying Kinds of Pronouns

Identify the boldfaced pronoun in each of the following sentences by writing **reflexive, intensive, demonstrative, indefinite, interrogative,** or **relative** on the line.

1. The class president, **who** just left office, was extremely effective. _____

2. **Whose** is this $50 bill on the floor? _____

3. Paul is a person **whom** everyone admires. _____

4. Marilyn saw **herself** reflected in the store window. _____

5. The students **themselves** decorated the gym for the dance. _____

6. **This** is an incredible story. _____

7. **Neither** of the books was available at the library. _____

8. **Which** of the ice cream flavors does Tammy prefer? _____

9. The mayor **herself** answered the reporters' questions. _____

10. The accused chose to defend **himself** at the trial. _____

11. **Most** of the customers paid with a credit card. _____

12. **Everyone** was amazed by the magician's disappearing act. _____

B. Using Pronouns

Complete each sentence with the type of pronoun specified in parentheses. Write the pronoun on the line.

1. Janet (intensive) _____ repaired the computer.

2. The Kaufmans painted their house and garage by (reflexive) _____.

3. I took these photos; Dino took (demonstrative) _____.

4. (Interrogative) _____ borrowed my ruler?

5. Karen met the author (relative) _____ book we are reading.

6. The books (relative) _____ I enjoy most are mysteries.

7. (Indefinite) _____ of the club members have paid their annual dues.

8. The artist (intensive) _____ explained the painting to us.

9. We have apple and cherry pie; (interrogative) _____ do you want for dessert?

10. I climbed the mountain to prove to (reflexive) _____ that I could do it.

For use with Pupil's Edition pp. 11–13

Other Kinds of Pronouns

Application

A. Writing with Pronouns

Write sentences about a discovery or invention that you feel was most useful to you in your daily life. In each sentence, use the type of pronoun indicated in parentheses. Underline the required pronoun in each sentence.

1. (indefinite pronoun) _____

_____

2. (demonstrative pronoun) _____

_____

3. (interrogative pronoun) _____

_____

4. (reflexive pronoun) _____

_____

5. (relative pronoun) _____

_____

6. (intensive pronoun) _____

_____

B. Writing a Story with Pronouns

Imagine that you were on the first expedition to the South Pole. Use the following pronouns in an original story about your experiences. Underline the pronouns in your story.

interrogative pronouns *who* and *whom;* reflexive pronoun *myself;* intensive pronoun *ourselves;* demonstrative pronoun *those;* indefinite pronoun *some;* relative pronoun *that.*

_____

_____

_____

_____

_____

_____

Lesson 4

Verbs

Reteaching

A **verb** is a word used to express an action, a condition, or a state of being.

An **action verb** expresses a physical or mental action. An action verb that appears with a direct object (a person or thing that receives the action of the verb) is called a **transitive verb.** An action verb without a direct object is an **intransitive verb.**

A **linking verb** links the subject of a sentence to a word in the predicate. Some linking verbs are forms of *be*, such as *am, is, was,* and *were.* Others, such as *appear, become, feel, look, remain, sound,* and *taste,* express conditions. Some verbs can be either action or linking verbs.

Auxiliary verbs, also called **helping verbs,** are combined with verbs to form **verb phrases,** such as *would have been climbing.* Some common auxiliary verbs are forms of *be* and *had, do, might, would, will, must, could,* and *would.*

A. Identifying Verbs

Underline the verb or verb phrase in each sentence. In the space above each verb, write **A** if it is an action verb, **L** if it is a linking verb, or **AUX** if it is an auxiliary verb.

1. Edmund Hillary and Tenzing Norgay climbed Mount Everest in 1953.

2. Hillary had been a professional beekeeper.

3. His fellow climber, Norgay, was a Sherpa from Nepal.

4. Tibetans call Mount Everest "The Goddess Mother of the World."

5. The mountain was named after Sir George Everest, a British surveyor.

6. Mount Everest straddles the border between Nepal and Tibet.

7. Everest towers above every other mountain on the earth.

8. Both Hillary and Norgay used oxygen tanks in the thin mountain air.

9. They could rise at a rate of only one foot per minute.

10. The climbers placed two items at the summit: a gift of chocolate to the Buddhist gods and a crucifix.

B. Identifying Transitive and Intransitive Verbs

Underline the verb or verb phrase in each sentence. If the verb has a direct object, underline it twice. On the line, write **T** for a transitive verb and **I** for an intransitive verb.

1. The summit loomed in the distance. _____

2. Many artists find inspiration in mountains. _____

3. The mountain casts its shadow over the sleepy town. _____

4. Even the mightiest mountain will erode over time. _____

5. The mountain goat scrambled up the slope. _____

For use with Pupil's Edition pp. 14–16

Lesson 4 **Verbs**   *More Practice*

A. Identifying Verbs

Underline each verb once. If the verb has a direct object, underline the direct object twice. On the line, write **T** for transitive and **I** for intransitive.

1. The tall building swayed slightly in the strong wind. _____

2. The caterpillar crawled slowly across the road. _____

3. The principal distributed attendance prizes at the awards ceremony. _____

4. Who knows the solution to the problem? _____

5. The audience applauded loudly at the end of the play. _____

6. Acid rain caused the deterioration of the outdoor statuary. _____

7. Not one student answered the question correctly. _____

8. The circus train arrived in town early in the morning. _____

9. The shark swam silently, with unblinking eyes. _____

10. The counselor called three students to her office. _____

B. Using Action and Linking Verbs

Complete each of the following sentences with an appropriate action or linking verb. Then, on the line to the right, identify each verb you have used by writing **A** for action or **L** for linking.

1. Mountain climbers _____ carefully for their trips. _____

2. The view from the summit _____ very beautiful. _____

3. Mountain climbing _____ a very dangerous sport. _____

4. Edmund Hillary _____ to the top of Mount Everest. _____

5. The climbers _____ the peak in late morning. _____

6. Very few people _____ such a trek. _____

7. K2 _____ the second highest mountain in the world. _____

8. Cindy _____ of climbing a cliff on every continent. _____

9. For such a quiet guy, John _____ very daring on a climb. _____

10. Dangerous icefalls _____ a menacing threat. _____

11. Sherpas _____ in Tibet and Nepal. _____

12. In 1954, an Italian expedition _____ K2. _____

CHAPTER 1

Lesson 4 Verbs

Application

A. Writing with Transitive and Intransitive Verbs

Use a form of each of the verbs listed below in two sentences, first as an
intransitive verb and then as a transitive verb.

> **EXAMPLE** move (intransitive) *That dancer moves gracefully.*
> (transitive) *Move that chair out of the way.*

1. **read:** (intransitive) _____

   (transitive) _____

2. **play:** (intransitive) _____

   (transitive) _____

3. **dance:** (intransitive) _____

   (transitive) _____

4. **see:** (intransitive) _____

   (transitive) _____

5. **grow:** (intransitive) _____

   (transitive) _____

6. **eat:** (intransitive) _____

   (transitive) _____

B. Proofreading

The writer of this paragraph was careless and omitted many verbs. Wherever a verb
is missing, insert this proofreading symbol ʌ and write an action verb, a linking verb,
or an auxiliary verb above it.

> The Rocky Mountains run from Alaska to New Mexico. The crest of the
>
> mountain range forms the Continental Divide, which separates streams that
>
> run to the east from streams that to the west. These streams the beginnings
>
> of many major rivers. The Rockies presented an obstacle to 19th-century
>
> pioneers. The travelers faced treacherous conditions on mountain passes.
>
> Some pioneers the highest mountains, traveling around them on the Santa Fe
>
> Trail, because they feared the dangerous mountain terrain. Today, in contrast,
>
> many people to the Rockies to enjoy winter sports. The Rockies an exciting
>
> tourist destination, but they us even now with their size and strength.

Copyright © McDougal Littell Inc.

For use with Pupil's Edition pp. 14–16

CHAPTER 1

Lesson 5 — Adjectives

Adjectives

Reteaching

Adjectives modify nouns or pronouns. They describe or give more specific information about the meaning of the nouns they modify. Adjectives tell *what kind, which one, how many,* or *how much.*

    <u>vibrant</u> color   <u>this</u> painting   <u>many</u> visitors   <u>more</u> fame

Articles are the most common adjectives. **Indefinite articles** (*a* and *an*) refer to unspecified members of groups of people, places, things, or ideas. *The* is the **definite article.** It refers to a specific person, place, thing, or idea.

Proper adjectives are formed from proper nouns. They are capitalized and often end with *-n, -an, -ian, -ese,* or *-ish*. Some examples are *Panamanian, Chinese,* and *Spanish*.

Finding Adjectives

Underline each adjective once and the word it modifies twice. Some words are modified by more than one adjective. Do not underline articles or possessive pronouns.

1. I have always appreciated good paintings and would love to own a huge collection by the biggest names in Western art.
2. The first artist I would pick is the incredible Leonardo da Vinci.
3. I believe he was the greatest artist of the Renaissance, the European revival of art and literature.
4. Da Vinci used perspective to create a three-dimensional space in a flat painting.
5. Perspective was a popular technique back then.
6. I would like a copy of the famous *Mona Lisa*, the mysterious woman with the teasing smile.
7. The next artist whose work I appreciate is the Italian painter called Titian.
8. Titian painted important people, including significant figures from the Bible or from classical Greek myths.
9. He also painted many portraits of wealthy people who paid him high fees.
10. The third painter I like is Jean-François Millet, a French artist who drew common people, not historical subjects.
11. Millet chose subdued shades for his paintings and avoided intense colors.
12. Next, I would choose some paintings by Paul Gauguin, who loved bright colors and exotic subjects.
13. Although Gauguin was a French citizen, he spent many years on the island of Tahiti.
14. Another French artist I like is Georges Seurat.
15. All of his pictures consist of tiny dots of pure color.
16. Because of his time-consuming style, he painted few pictures.
17. The overall effect of his paintings is enchanting.
18. Jackson Pollock's abstract paintings would be an interesting addition to my diverse collection.
19. His finished pictures are masses of dribbled and splattered paint.

Lesson 5

Adjectives

More Practice

A. Identifying Adjectives

Underline each adjective once and the word it modifies twice. Some words are modified by more than one adjective. Do not underline articles. If the adjective is a proper adjective, circle it, too.

1. One crisp, autumn day in 1879, Don Marcellino de Sautuola was taking a walk with his young daughter.

2. They were walking near the Spanish town of Santander.

3. Don Marcellino headed toward the caves near Altamira where he had found bones and small pieces of flint four years earlier.

4. This time he found nothing and was preparing to leave when he heard the loud shouts of his daughter from some secret, dark place within the cave.

5. The little girl was staring at breathtaking pictures on the smooth roof of the cave.

6. Don Marcellino saw pictures of animals similar to the American bison.

7. These paintings were of huge animals, drawn with great skill and amazing detail.

8. Many paintings of more animals—deer, wild boar, and running horses—covered the ceiling and walls.

9. Some animals appeared in three vivid colors.

10. Don Marcellino realized these incredible pictures had been painted by prehistoric artists.

11. At that time, most experts dismissed the paintings as forgeries because of the realistic pictures and the vivid colors.

12. No one knows why prehistoric people painted these wonderful pictures.

B. Using Adjectives

Fill in the blanks with one or more adjectives to improve the descriptions of the mystery-story characters presented below.

The butler has gray, wavy hair and wears a faded jacket with a button missing. Lady Margery wears expensive jewelry and has a resonant voice.

(1) Lord James wears suits and scarves, and he is surprisingly

_____: Penelope walks with tiny steps and wears her auburn

hair in tight curls. **(2)** The maid wears a _____ uniform, and

she speaks in a _____ voice. **(3)** Mr. Lunt is old, with

_____ skin. **(4)** The visitor from the United States has

_____ hair, _____ eyes, and a

_____ laugh. Agatha has a mischievous smile, a messy

appearance, and tangled hair. **(5)** Dr. Wooster seems quite _____.

For use with Pupil's Edition pp. 17–19

Lesson 5

Adjectives

Application

A. Writing Sentences with Adjectives

Revise these plain sentences by adding at least one adjective to each. You may also change articles as needed and add descriptive phrases and clauses. Write your new sentence on the line. Underline the adjectives you have added.

EXAMPLE   I hung the picture.

I hung the <u>colorful</u> picture on the <u>plain</u> wall of my bedroom.

1. A group of people visited the art museum.

_____

2. They saw a landscape of a mountain, trees, and a lake.

_____

3. People liked the colors in the paintings.

_____

4. The museum had a collection of pottery from Greece.

_____

5. One room was filled with statues.

_____

B. Revising with Adjectives

Read this simple paragraph. Then revise it, using adjectives to make its meaning clearer and more accurate. You may add phrases, clauses, or sentences as you wish. Write your new paragraph on the lines.

I decided to make a vase with pictures of butterflies on it. I slapped the clay on the potter's wheel, and, as the wheel started to spin, I attempted to mold the clay into a vase. Somehow, my vase turned into a bowl. I started to paint the butterflies, but the paint ran. My vase with butterflies had become a bowl with streaks.

_____

_____

_____

_____

_____

_____

_____

_____

CHAPTER 1

Lesson 6

Adverbs

Reteaching

Adverbs modify verbs, adjectives, or other adverbs. They answer the questions *where, when, how,* and *to what extent.* Adverbs are often formed by adding *–ly* to an adjective.

   arrived <u>here</u>   came <u>rather early</u>   ran <u>swiftly</u>   <u>almost</u> empty

An **intensifier** is an adverb that defines the degree of an adjective or another adverb. Intensifiers always precede the adjectives or adverbs they modify.

   <u>quite</u> ridiculous   <u>very</u> carefully

Finding Adverbs

Underline all the adverbs in the following sentences.

1. People have always watched the sky attentively.

2. Many study the heavens carefully in hopes they can accurately predict the weather that will arrive tomorrow.

3. One element that people look for anxiously is a storm.

4. There are people who are drawn irresistibly to storms.

5. Some "storm-chasers" study storms scientifically to learn more about storms than we know today.

6. Others chase storms to catch them vividly and dramatically on film.

7. Warren Faidley is a photographer who spends his life intentionally trying to get close to storms.

8. He started by going out on stormy nights and attempting, again and again, to take pictures of lightning.

9. He studied storms seriously and photographed them everywhere he could.

10. Storms are caused by annual weather patterns that are consistently found in the same areas of the country.

11. Warren is always traveling back and forth across the United States.

12. He stops in the areas most likely to be hit by storms.

13. His job often involves truly dangerous situations.

14. In 1987, he was knocked down forcefully by an extremely powerful lightning bolt.

15. He still managed to follow the storm and capture one of the most spectacular lightning strikes ever recorded.

16. On an incredibly stormy day in May 1993, Warren managed to photograph seven tornadoes successfully.

17. In 1992, Warren headed east to photograph Hurricane Andrew.

18. Warren drove into Miami, passing people moving inland, away from the danger.

19. He took photos while the wind blew loudly and violently around him.

20. His pictures show a city heavily damaged by a very destructive storm.

21. Warren is justifiably concerned about people who think storm-chasing is simply a recreational activity.

22. Warren is always cautious when a storm is near and never underestimates a storm's power.

For use with Pupil's Edition pp. 20–22

Lesson 6 **Adverbs**   *More Practice*

A. Identifying Adverbs

Underline each adverb once and the word it modifies twice in each of the following sentences.

1. The YTV director immediately replayed the footage of the field goal.

2. Kent seemed absolutely certain about the outcome of the test.

3. Robots perform many industrial tasks daily.

4. Isadora Duncan often interpreted human experience through dance.

5. Wait for us outside on the library steps.

6. Many psychiatrists today use the ink-blot test for personality analysis.

7. The Mediterranean Sea can look quite green from a distance.

8. A warm fire beckoned the travelers inside.

9. Can meteorologists predict weather accurately?

10. Sarah worked hard for her promotion to assistant manager.

B. Identifying Adverbs

Look at the boldfaced adverbs. Underline the word the adverb modifies. Then, on the line, tell whether the adverb is modifying a **V** (verb), an **ADJ** (adjective), or an **ADV** (adverb).

1. A tornado is an **extremely** destructive storm. _____

2. It can **quite** easily uproot large trees. _____

3. Tornadoes occur **almost** always in the United States. _____

4. A tornado starts as a **violently** rotating column of air. _____

5. This column of air, called a funnel cloud, **gradually** extends toward the earth. _____

6. If the funnel touches the ground, it **officially** becomes a tornado. _____

7. In the Northern Hemisphere, the winds of a tornado whirl **counterclockwise.** _____

8. If a tornado arrives in your area, go **immediately** to a shelter. _____

9. Some people act **very** foolishly by refusing to take shelter. _____

10. Blizzards are another **really** devastating storm. _____

11. In the United States, they occur **most** frequently in the northern Great Plains. _____

12. A blizzard is a blinding snowstorm with **intensely** strong winds. _____

13. The snowflakes begin drifting **rather** gently. _____

14. The snowflakes form huge snowdrifts, which can **completely** disrupt daily life. _____

15. Blizzards can make transportation **nearly** impossible. _____

Lesson 6

Adverbs

Application

A. Writing Sentences with Adverbs

Revise each of these sentences by adding at least one adverb. You may also add descriptive phrases and clauses if you wish. Write your new sentence on the line. Underline the adverbs you have added.

EXAMPLE The wind blew.
The wind blew underlined{insistently} all night.

1. Winter days are cold.

_____

2. The snow melted.

_____

3. Lightning struck the tall building.

_____

4. A tornado will smash everything in its path.

_____

5. The clouds floated in the sky.

_____

B. Writing with Adverbs

This paragraph is a first-person account of an ice storm. The account could be improved by the addition of adverbs. On the lines below, rewrite each numbered sentence. Include an adverb that modifies the boldfaced verb.

   The storm struck unexpectedly. One moment, white clouds floated deceptively overhead. The next moment, they broke. **(1)** I watched hailstones **drop.** In a few seconds, there was a thick coating of ice on streets and sidewalks. **(2)** Like animals from an ice forest, parked cars **crouched.** There was only the drumming of the hail for several minutes. Then a noise burst the air. **(3)** The air **crackled** as a power line leaned on a fence. **(4)** Police officers **drove** along the icy streets in response to accident calls. **(5)** I **realized** that my neighborhood might fit in on another planet, an ice planet. All landmarks seemed carved out of ice.

_____

_____

_____

_____

_____

_____

Lesson 7

Prepositions

Reteaching

CHAPTER 1

A **preposition** shows the relationship between a noun or pronoun and another word in the sentence. Some common prepositions include the following: *about, before, by, during, on,* and *under.* Prepositions formed from more than one word are **compound prepositions.** Some examples of compound prepositions are *according to, in place of, because of,* and *instead of.*

A **prepositional phrase** consists of a preposition, its object, and any modifiers of the object. The **object of the preposition** is the noun or pronoun that follows the preposition.

> The invention <u>of the telephone</u> changed life <u>around the world</u>. (*Of* and *around* are prepositions. *Telephone* and *world* are the objects of the prepositions.)

Finding Prepositions

Underline the preposition in each sentence. Remember that compound prepositions have two or more words. Underline the object or objects of the preposition twice.

1. The students in Mr. Lin's class were having an argument.
2. They were arguing about inventions.
3. According to one group, the telephone was obviously the most important.
4. "The telephone enables communication across the country and even the world!" insisted Mary.
5. "I am thinking of the refrigerator," countered Zach.
6. "I would not enjoy summer without ice cream and popsicles."
7. Scott declared, "How can you consider anything except the car?"
8. "Prior to the car, travel was extremely difficult and time-consuming."
9. "I vote for the elevator," said Darrell.
10. "Because of elevators, people could build skyscrapers."
11. "In spite of your arguments, I think the most useful invention is the computer," asserted Heather.
12. "On account of the computer and the Internet, we can send and receive information instantly."
13. Troy responded, "Television must rank among the top inventions."
14. "Television provides us with entertainment and the latest news."
15. Linda stated, "I put the printing press above every other invention."
16. "The printing press has spread knowledge throughout the world."
17. "Think of how we depend upon medical advancements!" Molly contributed.
18. "Using an X-ray, we can see through skin and muscles."
19. "I choose a simple invention, the zipper, over a complicated one," said Terry.
20. "We won't decide on one invention, so let's eat lunch," said Mr. Lin, and finally everyone agreed.

Copyright © McDougal Littell Inc.

Prepositions

More Practice

A. Identifying Prepositional Phrases

Underline each prepositional phrase once. Underline the object of the preposition twice. A sentence may have more than one prepositional phrase.

1. In 1945, an electronics genius named Percy Spencer was touring a lab.
2. He stopped in front of a magnetron, a power tube that emits microwave radiation.
3. Spencer realized that a chocolate bar in his pocket had started melting.
4. He was curious, and he did what any good inventor would do—he asked for a bag of popcorn.
5. Spencer did not feel like a snack; he wanted the popcorn for an experiment.
6. When he held the bag near a magnetron, the popcorn exploded all over the lab.
7. From this experiment Spencer and other scientists at the lab developed the microwave oven.
8. The first microwave ovens weighed over 700 pounds, stood five feet tall, and cost about 500 dollars.
9. Because of their size and cost, these microwave ovens were used in restaurants, railroad cars, and ocean liners.
10. Despite these drawbacks, research continued, and today the microwave oven is in millions of homes throughout the world.

B. Writing with Prepositional Phrases

Add a prepositional phrase to each sentence using the preposition specified in parentheses. Write your new sentence on the line.

EXAMPLE The computer crashed. (during)
The computer crashed during the thunderstorm.

1. The telephone rang. (for)

_____

2. I forgot the title. (of)

_____

3. Mrs. Hammett drove the car. (to)

_____

4. The house is 100 years old. (with)

_____

5. Denise saw that movie. (at)

_____

6. The pilot flew the plane. (above)

_____

For use with Pupil's Edition pp. 23–25

CHAPTER 1

Lesson 7

Prepositions

Application

A. Writing with Prepositional Phrases

Replace the prepositional phrase in each sentence. Write your new sentence on the line. Use a different preposition and a new object of the preposition.

> EXAMPLE   The tulips grew **by the garden path**.
> *The tulips grew in bright sunlight.*

1. The team practiced every day **before the meet**.

   _____

2. Paul played soccer **instead of baseball**.

   _____

3. My teacher recommended a book **about ancient Egypt**.

   _____

4. We bought some popcorn **during the intermission**.

   _____

5. The library is **between City Hall and the police station**.

   _____

6. The majority voted **against the tax increase**.

   _____

B. Writing with Prepositional Phrases

Use all of these prepositional phrases in an original story. Write your story on the lines below.

under my bed	instead of my keys	except her brother
behind the door	toward the mountain	despite my fear
after breakfast	because of her name	onto the roof

_____

_____

_____

_____

_____

_____

_____

Lessons 8–9 # Conjunctions and Interjections *Reteaching*

A **conjunction** connects words or groups of words.

A **coordinating conjunction** connects words or word groups that have equal importance in a sentence. The following are coordinating conjunctions: *and, but, for, nor, or, so,* and *yet.*

Correlative conjunctions are word pairs that join words or groups of words. Some correlative conjunctions are *both . . . and, either . . . or, not only . . . but also,* and *whether . . . or.*

Subordinating conjunctions introduce subordinate clauses—clauses that cannot stand alone as complete sentences. They join subordinate clauses to independent clauses—clauses that can stand alone as complete sentences. The following are some subordinating conjunctions: *after, because, if, so that, since, than, when,* and *while.*

A **conjunctive adverb** is used to express relationships between independent clauses. Some common conjunctive adverbs are *finally, furthermore, however, instead,* and *still.*

An **interjection** is a word or phrase that expresses a feeling. A strong interjection is followed by an exclamation point. A mild interjection is set off with commas.

Identifying Conjunctions, Conjunctive Adverbs, and Interjections

In the following sentences, underline the conjunctions once and the conjunctive adverbs twice. Draw parentheses around any interjections.

1. Neither my grandmother nor my grandfather had ever left their hometown.

2. They wanted to see more of the world; therefore, they decided to visit New York City.

3. When they saw New York, both my grandmother and grandfather said, "Wow!"

4. They were amazed not only by the tall buildings but also by the quick pace of life.

5. They had trouble deciding whether to travel by bus or by subway; consequently, they spent a lot of time either walking or taking taxis.

6. Soon they found that getting around in the city was easier than they had expected.

7. While they were in New York, they wanted to go to a few shows, for the arts are very popular there; accordingly, they bought tickets to a Broadway play and a jazz concert.

8. As they walked out of the theater after seeing the play, Grandma said, "Fantastic!"

9. They discussed whether they should go to the zoo or an art museum.

10. Since they love sports, they bought tickets to a baseball game.

11. They enjoyed Italian dinners, and they sampled Chinese food; however, Grandpa's favorite was a hot dog from a street vendor.

12. Their visit was not long, yet they managed to see a lot of the city.

13. Their trip had been exciting; furthermore, it had been a lot of fun.

For use with Pupil's Edition pp. 26–29

Lessons 8–9

Conjunctions and Interjections

More Practice

A. Identifying Conjunctions, Conjunctive Adverbs, and Interjections

In the following sentences, underline the conjunctions once and the conjunctive adverbs twice. Draw parentheses around any interjection.

1. All cities have some things in common, yet most big cities have unique landmarks.

2. Not only is Washington, D.C., our nation's capital, but it is also the home of many beautiful monuments.

3. Although the Opera House in Sydney, Australia, was originally not very popular, it has become the city's symbol; similarly, Parisians disliked the Eiffel Tower at first.

4. Amazing! The wrought-iron tower was once the world's highest structure.

5. San Francisco has both the Golden Gate Bridge and cable cars. Wow!

6. The Statue of Liberty and the Empire State Building are in New York City.

7. Unbelievable! It looks as though the Leaning Tower of Pisa will fall over any minute.

8. Neither time nor floods have diminished the beauty of St. Mark's Square in Venice; consequently, the square attracts thousands of visitors each year.

9. I haven't traveled extensively, but I can name several places I'd like to visit someday.

10. Provided I have the time and money, I will travel around the world.

B. Using Conjunctions, Conjunctive Adverbs, and Interjections

Complete the following sentences with a conjunction, a conjunctive adverb, or an interjection.

EXAMPLE We put an ad in the newspaper, *yet* nobody responded.

1. Ted _____ his brother went camping.

2. We drove slowly _____ the roads were icy.

3. We didn't have enough money; _____ we couldn't buy tickets.

4. I don't know _____ I'll take physics _____ chemistry next year.

5. _____! We're going to be late!

6. Mia is _____ an excellent soccer player _____ a great role model.

7. The movie was even better _____ we expected.

8. I have a bad cough; _____, I would go to the play with you.

9. Turn up the volume _____ I can hear the music.

10. _____! I burned my finger!

CHAPTER 1

Conjunctions and Interjections   *Application*

A. Writing a Diary Entry with Conjunctions and Interjections

Suppose that one day you visited an exciting city for the first time. On the lines
below, write a diary entry for that day. Use at least two coordinating conjunctions,
two correlative conjunctions, one subordinating conjunction, one conjunctive
adverb, and two interjections. Write the words you used under the appropriate
headings below your diary entry.

_____

_____

_____

_____

_____

_____

Coordinating Conjunctions   **Subordinating Conjunction**

_____   _____

_____

Correlative Conjunctions   **Conjunctive Adverb**

_____   _____

_____

Interjections

_____

_____

B. Using Conjunctions and Interjections in Writing

Revise the following paragraph, adding appropriate conjunctions and conjunctive
adverbs where they are needed. Add at least two interjections.

We had three maps of Los Angeles _____ we lost all of

them. _____! Most of us wanted to stop and ask for directions;

_____, my Dad said he could find his way around the city by

himself. That was a big mistake! Los Angeles is a city of complicated

freeways _____ about two million cars. _____ my

Mom _____ I wanted to see Mann's Chinese Theatre,

_____ we did not visit it _____ we could not find

it. _____! We were really lost! We drove around for about two

hours; _____ we stopped at a tourist center.

For use with Pupil's Edition pp. 26–29

Lesson 1

Simple Subjects and Predicates

Reteaching

Every sentence has two basic parts: the subject and the predicate.

The **simple subject** is the key word or words that tell who or what the sentence is about. The simple subject does not include modifiers. The **simple predicate,** or **verb,** is the principal word or group of words in the predicate. The verb phrase may consist of more than one word and may be interrupted by modifiers.

The <u>director</u> <u>explained</u> the upcoming scene.
SIMPLE   SIMPLE
SUBJECT   PREDICATE

<u>Lisa</u> <u>does</u> not <u>enjoy</u> horror films.
SIMPLE   SIMPLE
SUBJECT PREDICATE

Identifying Simple Subjects and Simple Predicates

Underline the simple subject once and the simple predicate twice.

EXAMPLE The <u>actors</u> <u>study</u> their lines for hours.

1. The cinematographer arranges the lighting for a film.
2. Another concern of the cinematographer is the quality of the photography.
3. Color film has been used since the 1940s.
4. Color film can make films more realistic.
5. Computer technology has permitted the colorization of black and white movies.
6. Two filmmakers may approach the same story with totally different results.
7. The advent of sound led to more realistic, less exaggerated acting.
8. In silent movies, subtitles communicated nonvisual information to the audience.
9. Today, foreign language movies with English subtitles can provide a similar experience.
10. Contemporary moviegoers readily accept sound effects as part of a film's atmosphere and mood.
11. Engineers must reproduce even the softest sounds accurately.
12. Sound effects are often experienced at a subconscious level.
13. The genre of musicals has been largely an American film phenomenon.
14. *Text* refers to the words in a script.
15. *Subtext* refers to the ideas and emotions behind the words in the script.
16. Experienced actors can interpret a single line in the script with a variety of emotions.
17. Often the most important scene in a film is the last one.
18. Some movies are filmed on location in exotic places all over the world.
19. Other movies are shot in studios with elaborate sets and lighting techniques.
20. Movie critics have become part of popular culture.
21. Critics' opinions serve as guides for millions of moviegoers.
22. Films may be adapted from other works of literature.

CHAPTER 2

Lesson 1

Simple Subjects and Predicates

More Practice

A. Identifying Simple Subjects and Simple Predicates

Underline the simple subject once and the simple predicate twice in each of the following sentences.

> **EXAMPLE** Good film <u>critics</u> <u>awaken</u> our curiosity.

1. Actors must commit many pages of a script to memory.
2. Critics rarely agree on the quality of films.
3. They react to films from their own tastes and perspectives.
4. Film techniques such as flashbacks may confuse the viewer.
5. Movies are surely the most expensive artistic expression!
6. Film has been used for both entertainment and education.
7. Publicity photos of actors and actresses show them in full make-up and costume.
8. Promotional movie posters are now their own art form.
9. Collectors of original movie posters often pay high prices for these works of art.
10. The skill of the editor contributes to any film's artistic and commercial success.

B. Identifying Complete Sentences

Some of the following items are complete sentences and some are fragments. If the item is a complete sentence, write **S** on the line. If the item is a fragment, write either **MSS** or **MSP** to identify whether the sentence is missing a simple subject or a simple predicate, or verb.

1. Spoke the first line of the lengthy script in a hushed voice. _____

2. Many films of the 1960s reflect either the violence of war or the mixed feelings of our citizens regarding war. _____

3. Filmmakers must be concerned with the rising costs of production. _____

4. Issues of right and wrong in modern society. _____

5. Film actors constantly in the public eye. _____

6. Began his career as a child star in the 1940s. _____

7. A versatile actor at home on stage, television, and film. _____

8. Has been left on the cutting-room floor. _____

9. Remember that the term *fan* comes from the word *fanatic*. _____

10. Actors under exclusive contract with allegiance to only one film company. _____

11. A respected star of stage and screen for more than a decade. _____

12. The word *Hollywood* is synonymous with American movies. _____

For use with Pupil's Edition pp. 38–39

Simple Subjects and Predicates

Application

A. Writing Subjects and Predicates

Write sentences on the lines below by adding both a subject and a predicate to each fragment. Do not use the fragment as the subject of the sentence.

> **EXAMPLE** under the actor's make-up
> *The human flaws were hidden under the actor's make-up.*

1. nearly a million fan letters _____

_____

2. elaborate sets for historical films _____

_____

3. can take viewers to fantastic and imaginary worlds _____

_____

4. danced with the leading man, a famous star _____

_____

5. his physical appearance _____

_____

6. several actors in heavy armor _____

_____

B. Revising

Read this paragraph carefully. It contains several sentence fragments. When you find a sentence fragment, insert this proofreading symbol ∧ and write a subject or a predicate in the space above it.

> **EXAMPLE** Good ∧ must become their characters.
>   *actors*

Hollywood the center of the movie industry. Filmmakers, producers, directors, cameramen, stunt men, make-up artists, costume designers, and scores of other workers related to the business of making films. Nearby Beverly Hills one of the fashion meccas of the world. Much of the economy of the greater Los Angeles area. Actors and actresses from the East Coast. Movie-lovers by its charms. Visitors to the film studios. On studio tours, may experience firsthand some of the special effects involved in filmmaking. Visitors leave the city, taking with them some of the excitement of the movies. When they see the large letters on the hillside that spell H-O-L-L-Y-W-O-O-D.

Lesson 2

Complete Subjects and Predicates

Reteaching

The **complete subject** includes the simple subject and all the words that modify it. The **complete predicate** includes the verb and all the words that modify it. Every word in a sentence is either part of the complete subject or part of the complete predicate.

<u>Rock music</u> <u>evolved from rhythm and blues and country music</u>.

COMPLETE
SUBJECT

COMPLETE PREDICATE

A. Identifying Complete Subjects and Complete Predicates

Underline the complete subject once and the complete predicate twice.

> **EXAMPLE** <u>Early rock fans</u> <u>enjoyed the music of Chuck Berry and Bill Haley.</u>

1. Early rocker Chuck Berry was known for his inventive guitar work.
2. Bill Haley and the Comets brought the sound of rock to a wide audience.
3. Most parents were not accustomed to the sound of this new music.
4. Some people opposed rock music violently.
5. The rhythms of rock were different from those of the big band era.
6. Even the major instruments differed from those featured in early '50s pop music.
7. The lead guitar, rhythm guitar, bass guitar, and drums replaced the big bands.
8. The rise of the Beatles made rock music truly international.
9. Fans from New York to California screamed with excitement at Beatles concerts.
10. The thrill of a rock concert remains the same for today's audiences.

B. Identifying Complete Subjects and Complete Predicates

Underline the complete subject once and the complete predicate twice. Then decide which part of the sentence the boldfaced word belongs to. Write **Part of subject** or **Part of predicate** on the line.

1. Huge trucks **roll** across the nation's highways all night long. _____

2. What percentage of **travelers** use telephone credit cards? _____

3. Some **poisonous** snakes have been found along this trail. _____

4. We stopped at the fast-food restaurant for a snack after the **dance.** _____

5. Eager travelers enjoyed the sight of maple trees with colorful **leaves.** _____

6. The **old** gas lamps cast a warm glow on the flowered wallpaper. _____

7. Why **have** you taken down your favorite poster? _____

8. The U.S. president travels **around** the world in *Air Force One*. _____

9. Unknown **vandals** damaged the statue in front of the art museum. _____

10. The damaged statue stands as a **reminder** of the effects of human violence. _____

For use with Pupil's Edition pp. 40–41

Lesson 2

Complete Subjects and Predicates

More Practice

A. Identifying Complete Subjects and Complete Predicates

Draw a vertical line between the complete subject and the complete predicate in each of the following sentences.

> **EXAMPLE** Country and western music | has its roots in southern folk music.

1. Groups such as the Carter family recorded old traditional ballads.

2. The family used vocal techniques and instruments typical of traditional folk music.

3. The Grand Ole Opry in Nashville showcases country music talent.

4. Audiences in the 1930s enjoyed music from the Grand Ole Opry in a national network radio show.

5. The lyrics of many country songs dwell on serious topics such as poverty and loneliness.

6. Listeners often identify with the emotions of the singers.

7. Many types of music can be classified as country music.

8. Traditional bluegrass music is a particularly pure form of country music.

9. Country rock has attracted many popular performers.

10. Country music offers a variety of styles for many tastes.

B. Using Complete Subjects and Complete Predicates

On the line to the right of each item, write how each of the following groups of words could be used: **CS** for a complete subject or **CP** for a complete predicate. Then use each group of words to write a complete sentence, adding a complete subject or complete predicate as necessary.

> **EXAMPLE** a cool glass of lemonade _____CS_____
> *A cool glass of lemonade would taste good right now.*

1. all members of the drama club _____

_____

2. flew past us _____

_____

3. big cats in zoos _____

_____

4. a beautiful blue heron _____

_____

5. need large cages or extensive fenced areas _____

_____

6. have made great progress _____

_____

CHAPTER 2

Lesson 2

Complete Subjects and Predicates

Application

A. Revising by Adding Details

Create more interesting sentences by adding details to the simple subjects and predicates below.

1. Birds fly.

_____

2. Inventors think.

_____

3. Politicians are arguing.

_____

4. Sources revealed.

_____

5. Planets rotate.

_____

6. Sharks eat.

_____

B. Writing with Complete Subjects and Complete Predicates

Imagine that you have taken these notes for a report. As you review your notes, rewrite fragments as complete sentences. Write the following notes as sentences that have complete subjects and predicates. If you like, you may combine two or more fragments in a single sentence.

Benny Goodman. Born in Chicago in 1909. Began clarinet lessons at the age of ten. A tremendous talent. Goodman, at the age of only 13. Played with dance orchestras. Formed his own band in 1934. Popular immediately. Became known as "King of Swing." Part of immensely popular dance band era. Remembered fondly by audiences who saw him long ago. Enjoyed by today's audiences.

_____

_____

_____

_____

_____

_____

_____

For use with Pupil's Edition pp. 40–41

Lesson 3 — Compound Sentence Parts

Reteaching

A **compound subject** is made up of two or more subjects that share a verb. The subjects are joined by a conjunction, or connecting word, such as *and, or,* or *but.*

<u>Books</u> and <u>magazines</u> <u>are sold</u> at the drugstore.

COMPOUND SUBJECT   SIMPLE VERB

A **compound verb** is made up of two or more verbs or verb phrases that are joined by a conjunction and have the same subject. They can also share a complement.

<u>Lynette</u> <u>buys</u> and <u>reads</u> many magazines.

SIMPLE   COMPOUND VERB
SUBJECT

A **compound predicate** is made up of a compound verb and all the words that go with each verb. In a compound predicate, the verbs do not share a complement.

The stock boy <u>opens boxes</u> and <u>puts items on the shelves.</u>

COMPLETE   COMPOUND PREDICATE
SUBJECT

Identifying Simple Subjects and Verbs

In each sentence, underline the simple subject(s) once and the verb(s) twice. Write **CS** if the sentence has a compound subject or **CV** if it has a compound verb. The sentences with compound predicates have already been identified.

    EXAMPLE The <u>druggist</u> <u>fills</u> prescriptions and <u>answers</u> questions. *CP*

1. Cold remedies and cough medicines are located on this shelf. _____

2. Customers want and expect good value for their dollar. _____

3. Cash and credit are accepted in most stores today. _____

4. Buyers research the public's desires and supply attractive merchandise *CP*

5. Store managers recruit and hire the best personnel available. _____

6. Students and retired persons often work as salesclerks. _____

7. That customer is returning a purchase and is buying an electric fan. *CP*

8. The cashier verifies the price of each item and works the cash register. *CP*

9. The quality of service makes or breaks a neighborhood store. _____

10. Customers tire of waiting in line and take their business to a more efficient store. *CP*

11. Drugs and cosmetics are part of most drugstores' inventory. _____

12. Birthday cards and party supplies are shelved beside each other. _____

13. Many drugstores compete for customers and offer special coupons. *CP*

For use with Pupil's Edition pp. 42–43

Lesson 3

Compound Sentence Parts

More Practice

A. Identifying Simple Subjects and Verbs

In each sentence, underline the simple subject(s) once and the verb(s) twice.

EXAMPLE <u>Orchestras</u> and <u>bands</u> <u><u>have</u></u> traditional places for the various instruments.

1. Trombones and trumpets are found at the rear of the orchestra.
2. The piano and the harp can always be found on the left-hand side of the orchestra semicircle.
3. Audience members can hear the instruments clearly and can appreciate the blend of sounds.
4. Conductors study and often memorize even complex musical scores.
5. Professional musicians concentrate on their own parts but also listen to the sound of the orchestra playing together.

B. Using Compound Subjects, Compound Verbs, and Compound Predicates

Combine the sentence pairs to form a new sentence with the sentence part indicated in parentheses. Use the conjunction—*and, or, nor,* or *but*—that makes the most sense.

EXAMPLE Hiking in the mountains can be dangerous. Skiing in them can be, too. (compound subject)
Hiking and skiing in the mountains can be dangerous.

1. The Saint Bernard is now a beloved pet. Once it was mainly a work dog. (compound predicate)

_____

2. Its ancestors were bred by Swiss monks. Its ancestors were named after the monastery where they were bred. (compound predicate)

_____

3. In the Swiss Alps, blinding snowstorms can jeopardize travelers and isolate villages. Deadly avalanches can do that, too. (compound subject and compound predicate)

_____

4. Travelers recognize these faithful dogs. Travelers welcome them. (compound verb)

_____

5. Folktales describe this powerful dog's rescue feats. Legends describe them. (compound subject)

_____

6. Storms did not keep this rugged rescuer from its job. Neither did avalanches. (compound subject)

_____

For use with Pupil's Edition pp. 42–43

Lesson 3

Compound Sentence Parts

Application

A. Sentence Combining with Compound Subjects, Compound Verbs, and Compound Predicates

Combine each pair of sentences by writing a compound subject, a compound verb, or a compound predicate. Be sure that the subject and the verb agree in number.

1. The furniture department in this store is large. The electronics department is large, too.

_____

2. Buyers for this department store travel around the world. They keep up with the latest fashions.

_____

3. Maura entered the store through the east door. She left by the same door.

_____

4. The store managers changed most of the departments on this floor. They left the shoe department in the same place.

_____

5. These sweaters come in small sizes. Those jackets come in small sizes, too.

_____

B. More Sentence Combining

Revise the following paragraph, using compound subjects, compound verbs, and compound predicates to combine sentences with similar ideas. Write the new paragraph on the lines below. Use a separate piece of paper if necessary.

When the mall opened, the face of shopping in our town changed dramatically. Boutiques opened there. Shoe stores opened there. Two new department stores opened there, too. Sandwich shops in the mall have become popular. A mid-priced restaurant has also become popular. Customers walk slowly down the mall. They study the window displays along the way. Customers price items. They compare them. They value the availability of a variety of goods. They shop for the best price. People enjoy the comfort of shopping in the new mall. They return again and again.

_____

_____

_____

_____

_____

CHAPTER 2

Lesson 4

Kinds of Sentences

Reteaching

A **declarative sentence** expresses a statement of fact, wish, intent, or feeling. It ends with a period.

> Scientists have identified at least 800,000 species of insect.

An **interrogative sentence** asks a question. It ends with a question mark.

> Do you know how many legs an insect has?

An **imperative sentence** gives a command, request, or direction. It usually ends with a period. If the command is strong, it may end with an exclamation point.

> Close the door quickly!

An **exclamatory sentence** expresses strong feeling. It always ends with an exclamation point.

> Watch out for that bee hive!

Identifying Kinds of Sentences

On the line, identify each sentence below by writing **DEC** for declarative, **INT** for interrogative, **IMP** for imperative, or **EXC** for exclamatory. Add the proper punctuation mark at the end of each sentence.

1. Every insect has six legs _____

2. Were you ever stung by a yellow jacket _____

3. Identify the type of insect crawling on the outside of this window _____

4. How colorful this beetle is _____

5. Insects are found everywhere—from the polar regions to the tropics _____

6. Some stick-like insects have wingspans of 12 inches _____

7. How amazing the variety of insects in the world is _____

8. Scientists are constantly discovering more species of insects, especially in the world's jungles _____

9. Why do some species such as bees and ants form complex social communities _____

10. Explain how these insects survive _____

11. The 17-year locust matures over a period of nearly 17 years _____

12. Do you know how long a common housefly lives _____

13. The difference between species is absolutely incredible _____

14. Some insects feed on only one type of plant _____

15. Imagine having only one item on your menu for your whole life _____

CHAPTER 2

For use with Pupil's Edition pp. 44–45

Lesson 4 Kinds of Sentences

More Practice

Using Different Kinds of Sentences

Add the correct end punctuation to each of these sentences. Then rewrite the sentences according to the instructions in parentheses. Use the same subject and verb. You may have to add or delete words and change word order.

> **EXAMPLE** That quarterback really throws long passes.
> (Change to a question.)
> *Does that quarterback throw long passes?*

1. Did you look at that unusual sports car
(Change to an imperative sentence.)

_____

2. Is the Amazon the longest river in the world
(Change to a declarative sentence.)

_____

3. Pick the apples when they are ripe
(Change to an interrogative sentence.)

_____

4. Is the boat sinking
(Change to an exclamatory sentence.)

_____

5. What an amazing story that was
(Change to a declarative sentence.)

_____

6. The stamp belongs in the upper right-hand corner of the envelope
(Change to an interrogative sentence.)

_____

7. How beautiful this sunset is
(Change to a declarative sentence.)

_____

8. Did you mail your application today
(Change to an imperative sentence.)

_____

9. Is there a spider on my back
(Change to an exclamatory sentence.)

_____

10. He will call me tonight with his answer
(Change to an interrogative sentence.)

_____

CHAPTER 2

Lesson 4 # Kinds of Sentences *Application*

A. Writing Different Kinds of Sentences in a Monologue

Imagine that you are a beekeeper who is showing visitors around her job site. Write a short speech that you might give, even if you actually know very little, or nothing at all, about beekeeping. Use at least one of each of the following types of sentences: declarative, interrogative, imperative, and exclamatory. Use the correct punctuation at the end of each sentence. Use a separate piece of paper if necessary.

_____

_____

_____

_____

_____

_____

_____

_____

_____

_____

B. Writing Different Kinds of Sentences in a Dialogue

Write a dialogue, or conversation, that two people on a picnic are having. Their picnic is being overrun with ants, bees, mosquitoes, or some other kinds of insects. Use at least one of each kind of sentence: declarative, interrogative, imperative, and exclamatory. Enclose each speaker's words in quotation marks. Use the correct punctuation at the end of each sentence, inside the quotation marks. Use a separate piece of paper if necessary.

_____

_____

_____

_____

_____

_____

_____

_____

For use with Pupil's Edition pp. 44–45

Lesson 5 # Subjects in Unusual Positions   *Reteaching*

In an **inverted sentence,** the subject appears after the verb or between the words that make up the verb phrase. An inverted sentence can be used for variety or emphasis.

> Out of the tree <u>flew</u> the <u>flock</u> of birds.
>   VERB   SUBJECT

When a sentence begins with the words *here* or *there*, the subject usually follows the verb. *Here* and *there* may be adverbs of place or expletives, which have no meaning of themselves.

> ADVERB OF PLACE   There <u>goes</u> the <u>flock</u>! (Where is the flock? *There*.)
>   VERB   SUBJECT

> EXPLETIVE   There <u>are</u> 20 <u>birds</u> in that flock. (*There* does not tell where.)
>   VERB SUBJECT

In a **question,** the subject usually appears after the verb or between the words that make up the verb phrase.

> <u>Are</u> <u>you</u> lost?   <u>Is</u> your <u>heart</u> <u>beating</u> fast?
> VERB SUBJECT   AUXILIARY   SUBJECT MAIN VERB
>   VERB

In an **imperative sentence,** the subject is *you*. Often, *you* is not stated.

> <u>Avoid</u> poison ivy.
> VERB   (understood SUBJECT is *You*.)

Finding Subjects and Verbs in Unusual Positions

In the following sentences, underline the simple subject once and the verb or verb phrase twice. If the subject is understood, write **You** in parentheses on the line.

1. With the damp, humid weather came mildew. _____

2. How much does sugar contribute to tooth decay? _____

3. Is Hawaii the most southerly state in this country? _____

4. Stop tapping your fingers on the table! _____

5. Under my bed were the missing keys. _____

6. Answer my question. _____

7. From somewhere in the back row came a burst of laughter. _____

8. There is an old campsite in the woods. _____

9. Only once before had the town staged a welcome-home parade. _____

10. Go to sleep now. _____

11. Here is a slice of freshly baked cherry pie. _____

12. In the audience sat talent scouts. _____

CHAPTER 2

Lesson 5

Subjects in Unusual Positions

More Practice

A. Writing Sentences

In the following sentences, underline the simple subject once and the verb twice. Then rewrite each sentence so that the subject comes before the verb.

> **EXAMPLE** Across the field <u>ran</u> the soccer <u>players</u>.
>
> *The soccer players ran across the field.*

1. There is the oldest schoolhouse in the state.

_____

2. In that house lived Paul Revere.

_____

3. Was the downtown traffic heavy today?

_____

4. In the wild live few pandas.

_____

5. Over the fence scrambled the frightened kitten.

_____

B. Writing Sentences

Rewrite each sentence as an inverted or imperative sentence. You may choose to add *Here* or *There*. Then underline each subject once and each verb twice in your new sentence.

> **EXAMPLE** The petunias grew in the flower box.
>
> *In the flower box <u>grew</u> the <u>petunias</u>.*

1. The tax forms are here.

_____

2. My brand new bike lay there in the mud.

_____

3. Seven spelling errors are in your essay.

_____

4. You will forget that phone number.

_____

5. Tourists were waiting on the dock.

_____

6. Your sister is moving to the college dorm.

_____

7. The sun shone above the clouds.

_____

For use with Pupil's Edition pp. 46–48

Lesson 5 # Subjects in Unusual Positions   *Application*

A. Revising Using a Variety of Sentence Orders

The writer of this paragraph decided never to use the traditional word order of subject before verb. In all of the paragraph's sentences, the subject is found in an unusual position or is understood. Rewrite the paragraph, this time using a variety of sentence orders to make the paragraph more understandable and pleasing to the reader. Use a separate piece of paper if necessary.

Most exciting was the book I read last weekend. From a galaxy far away came the invaders. Huge were their misshapen heads. Clumsy were their long bodies in Earth's heavy atmosphere. Why did they come to our planet? On their own planet lurked a dangerous enemy killer germ. There was no way to destroy it. So here was their last chance. Was their attack on unsuspecting humans successful? Did they take over Earth and its inhabitants? Read the book to find out the answers.

_____

_____

_____

_____

B. Revising Using a Variety of Sentence Orders

The writer of this paragraph decided always to use the traditional word order of subject before verb. Rewrite the paragraph, this time using a variety of sentences, including those arranged in the traditional order of subject before verb and at least two in which the verb comes before the subject. Use a separate piece of paper if necessary.

Lillie Coit was an unusual person in one way. Even as a child, she was fascinated by fire. Many wooden buildings were in San Francisco, Lillie's hometown. Too often, the fire alarm sounded. Immediately the firefighters sprang into action. Lillie sprang into action, too. She followed the firemen to the fires. Sometimes she would help when they were short-handed. She became the unofficial mascot of one group. Her father was not happy about her obsession. He moved her away from the city. But she was stubborn. She kept up her interest in her beloved firefighting. When she died, Lillie left the city of San Francisco a great deal of money. Coit Tower was built with that money and stands as a memorial to the city's brave firefighters.

_____

_____

_____

_____

Lesson 6

Subject Complements

Reteaching

Complements are words or groups of words that complete the meaning or action of verbs. **Subject complements** are words that follow linking verbs and describe or rename the subjects.

Predicate adjectives describe subjects by telling *which one, what kind, how much,* or *how many.*

> The plot was ridiculous.
>
> SUBJECT LINKING PREDICATE
> VERB ADJECTIVE

Predicate nominatives are nouns or pronouns that rename, identify, or define subjects.

> This play is a success.
>
> SUBJECT LINKING PREDICATE
> VERB NOMINATIVE

Identifying Linking Verbs and Subject Complements

In the following sentences, underline the linking verbs once and the subject complements twice. On the line, write **PA** for predicate adjective or **PN** for predicate nominative.

1. *Our Town* by Thornton Wilder was a strange play for its time. _____

2. At the beginning of the play, the stage is empty. _____

3. Audiences seemed confused at first. _____

4. They soon became more accustomed to the bare stage. _____

5. The characters in the play seem familiar to most audiences. _____

6. They are similar to people in every small, or big, town. _____

7. Thornton Wilder was sensitive to the beauty of everyday life. _____

8. Emily is a young girl in New Hampshire. _____

9. George is her next-door neighbor. _____

10. Friends at first, they soon become husband and wife. _____

11. Emily's mother and father are kind. _____

12. George's father is the town doctor. _____

13. Grover's Corners seems peaceful. _____

14. The people of Grover's Corners are down-to-earth folks. _____

15. To some people, the play is unrealistically sweet. _____

16. To most people, however, the play seems true. _____

17. *Our Town* was the winner of the 1938 Pulitzer Prize for drama. _____

18. It is a favorite choice for amateur theater groups. _____

For use with Pupil's Edition pp. 49–50

CHAPTER 2

Lesson 6

Subject Complements

More Practice

A. Identifying Types of Subject Complements

In each of the following sentences, underline the linking verb once and the subject complement twice. Then, in the blank, write **PN** if the subject complement is a **predicate nominative** or **PA** if it is a **predicate adjective.**

EXAMPLE My high-top sneakers <u>are</u> <u>comfortable</u>. __*PA*__

1. The Welsh pony is a small horse used in coal mines. _____

2. Vienna became justly famous for its porcelain and pastries. _____

3. Dick Whittington and his cat are much-loved English folk heroes. _____

4. This stand-up comedian is hilarious. _____

5. The reddest strawberries taste especially sweet. _____

6. Mrs. Rodriguez has become a crossing guard at her son's school. _____

7. Whispers sound loud in a quiet room. _____

8. My dog's fur feels smooth against my cheek. _____

9. His latest novel is a story about an international spy ring. _____

10. Stonehenge in England has been a tourist attraction for centuries. _____

B. Using Subject Complements

Complete each sentence below. First, complete it with a predicate nominative; then complete it with a predicate adjective.

EXAMPLE The play was _____*a comedy*_____.
The play was _____*unbelievable.*_____.

1. The playwright is _____.

   The playwright is _____.

2. The performance was _____.

   The performance was _____.

3. The pit band for the musical is _____.

   The pit band for the musical is _____.

4. The director is _____.

   The director is _____.

5. The review in the newspaper was _____.

   The review in the newspaper was _____.

Lesson 6

Subject Complements

Application

A. Writing Subject Complements

Rewrite each of the numbered sentences in the passage below with a new subject complement. Underline your new subject complement. If it is a predicate nominative, write **PN** in parentheses after the sentence. If it is a predicate adjective, write **PA.**

      (1) The dinner last night was a triumph. **(2)** The appetizers served before the main course were surprisingly flavorful. **(3)** The main course was absolutely delicious. **(4)** The dessert became an instant favorite. **(5)** After the meal, I felt fully satisfied. **(6)** That restaurant has become the top name on my list of great restaurants.

1. _____

2. _____

3. _____

4. _____

5. _____

6. _____

B. Writing with Subject Complements

A critic has just seen a play and has written a few quick notes about it. Use his notes to write six sentences with predicate adjectives for his review. Use words from the columns below. You may use each word only once, and you must use all the words. Add other words to make the sentences more interesting.

Nouns	Verbs	Adjectives
plot	was	loud
actors	were	expensive
stage	seemed	silly
props	sounded	uncomfortable
band	looked	crowded
tickets	seemed	inappropriate

1. _____

2. _____

3. _____

4. _____

5. _____

6. _____

For use with Pupil's Edition pp. 49–50

CHAPTER 2

Lesson 7 Objects of Verbs

Reteaching

A **direct object** is a word or a group of words that names the receiver of the action of an action verb. It answers the question *what* or *whom*.

My dog has a short <u>tail</u>. (My dog has *what*?)

An **indirect object** is a word or group of words that tells *to what, to whom,* or *for whom* an action is done. The indirect object almost always comes before the direct object in sentences that have both.

My dog brought <u>me</u> a stick. (*To whom* did the dog bring the stick?)

An **objective complement** is a word or group of words that follows a direct object and renames or describes that object. An objective complement may be a noun or an adjective.

Dog show judges named my dog a <u>champion</u>. (*champion* describes the direct object *dog*.)

Recognizing Objects of Verbs

In each sentence, if the underlined word is a direct object, write **DO** on the line. If it is an indirect object, write **IO**. If it is an objective complement, write **OC**.

EXAMPLE Our kitten takes <u>naps</u> throughout the day. _____*DO*_____

1. Japan named its deciduous cypress tree the umbrella <u>pine</u>. _____

2. The first jet engine brought <u>Frank Whittle</u> fame. _____

3. The judges named Steve the "<u>Rookie of the Year</u>" in soccer. _____

4. The Xhosa language of South Africa contains three different click <u>sounds</u>. _____

5. Villagers of New Guinea and West Africa grow <u>yams</u> as a staple food. _____

6. Mr. Ortega gave <u>us</u> a surprise quiz in trigonometry yesterday. _____

7. For four consecutive years, our class has elected Sandra its <u>president</u>. _____

8. The museum curators hung their new <u>masterpiece</u> in the main hall. _____

9. The basketball coach taught her players some new ball-handling <u>techniques</u>. _____

10. At the awards banquet, the coach gave <u>John</u> special recognition. _____

11. The children built a <u>snowman</u> in their front yard. _____

12. The noise from his CD player is driving me <u>crazy</u>. _____

13. Jean named her cat <u>Mehitabel</u> after a famous cat in fiction. _____

14. In a hushed voice, Rachel told the <u>campers</u> the story of the phantom hitchhiker. _____

15. Thomas Jefferson founded the <u>University of Virginia</u> in Charlottesville. _____

Objects of Verbs

More Practice

A. Identifying Objects of Verbs

Identify the function of the boldfaced word or words in each sentence below. Write **DO** for direct object, **IO** for indirect object, and **OC** for objective complement. If the word cannot be classified as the direct object, the indirect object, or the objective complement, write **N**.

    EXAMPLE The zoologist gave the **students** a lecture on cats. _____*IO*_____

1. Cats have a strong hunting **instinct**. _____

2. Housecats often bring their **owners** captured prey. _____

3. They expect praise for their **skill** at hunting. _____

4. Lions hunt their **prey** in the Serengeti National Park in Tanzania. _____

5. People often call the lion the **"king of beasts."** _____

6. Experts consider female lions better **hunters** than their male counterparts. _____

7. Female lions share their kill with male **lions.** _____

8. Lion parents teach their **offspring** how to hunt. _____

9. Lions find zebras a satisfying **meal**. _____

10. Lions in the midst of a hunt show their **prey** no mercy. _____

B. Using Indirect Objects

Underline the direct object in each sentence below. Then rewrite each sentence, adding an indirect object. Use a different indirect object for every sentence.

1. On my parents' anniversary, I made a wedding cake.

    _____

2. Show the findings of your research.

    _____

3. The gentleman offered his seat.

    _____

4. The resort manager sent an advertisement for her establishment.

    _____

5. That close call taught a lesson about the importance of seat belts.

    _____

6. Write a postcard when you reach your destination.

    _____

For use with Pupil's Edition pp. 51–53

Lesson 7 Objects of Verbs

Application

A. Using Objects of Verbs

Choose one word from each list below to complete each sentence. Use each word only once. Each sentence should have both an indirect object and a direct object. You can add words to make the sentences more interesting.

Use as indirect object	Use as direct object
her customer	a birthday card
the athlete	a lie
her grandsons	a story
his students	a big check
his buddies	climbing techniques
her babies	worms
his nephew	asylum
her aunt	today's edition

1. The mother bird brought _____.

2. Tracy sent _____.

3. The mountaineer taught _____.

4. The boastful fisherman told _____.

5. The paper carrier handed _____.

6. The embassy officials offered _____.

7. Grandma told _____.

8. The millionaire wrote _____.

B. Writing Sentences with Objects of Verbs

Complete each sentence with an objective complement—either a noun or an adjective.

EXAMPLE My little sister keeps me *busy all day.*

1. My family considers me _____.

2. One time I was appointed _____.

3. My best friend calls me _____.

4. When I was christened, I was named _____.

5. No one would ever call me _____.

6. My teachers consider me _____.

7. Most little children find me _____.

8. In a dream, I was chosen _____.

Lesson 8

Sentence Diagramming

More Practice 1

Complete each diagram with the sentence provided.

A. Simple Subjects and Predicates

Boats float.

B. Compound Subjects and Verbs

Compound Subject Canoes and kayaks float.

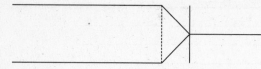

Compound Verb Boaters sit and paddle.

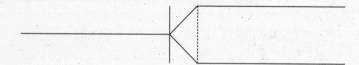

Compound Subject and Compound Verb Katy and Rob sit and paddle.

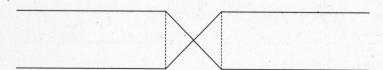

C. Adjectives and Adverbs

Adjectives and Adverbs The proficient boaters are paddling smoothly.

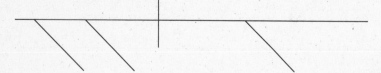

For use with Pupil's Edition pp. 54–57

CHAPTER 2

Lesson 8 **Sentence Diagramming**   *More Practice 2*

D. Direct Objects

Single Direct Object Rob owns a small canoe.

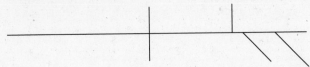

Compound Direct Object His parents own a larger canoe and a kayak.

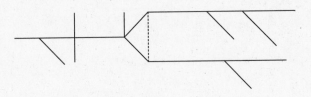

Compound Predicate The family likes the river and often takes canoe trips.

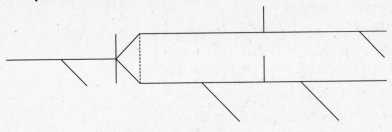

E. Indirect Objects

These trips give the whole family healthy entertainment.

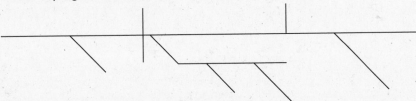

F. Objective Complements

Rob considers the canoe trips short vacations.

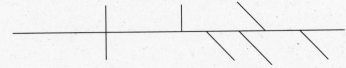

Lesson 8

Sentence Diagramming

Application

On another piece of paper, diagram each of these sentences.

A. Diagramming Subjects, Verbs, and Modifiers

1. The current moves quickly here.
2. Can you swim?
3. The energetic campers hiked and canoed.
4. Several campers and their counselors raced downstream.

B. Diagramming Complements and Objects

1. This canoe trip is my first one.
2. The counselors gave every camper a life jacket.
3. All the campers are having a great time.
4. That team named their canoe Topsy.

C. Mixed Practice

1. The daylong outing was absolutely perfect!
2. This state park runs an efficient boat-rental service.
3. We rode a truck uphill and canoed down.
4. The water looked somewhat rough.
5. The experienced boaters gave the first-timers helpful advice.
6. Boys and girls swam and dived.
7. Later, the hungry campers ate hot dogs and hamburgers.
8. Everyone considered the day a success.

For use with Pupil's Edition pp. 54–57

Lesson 1

Prepositional Phrases

Reteaching

A **prepositional phrase** consists of a preposition, its object, and any modifiers of the object.

> Have you ever played <u>in a band</u>? (The preposition is *in*.)

An **adjective phrase** is a prepositional phrase that modifies a noun or a pronoun. It usually tells *which one* or *what kind* about the word it modifies.

> The band <u>at our school</u> is small. (The phrase modifies *band*, telling which one.)

An **adverb phrase** is a prepositional phrase that modifies a verb, an adjective, or another adverb. It tells *how, when, where,* or *to what extent* about the word it modifies.

> The conductor motions <u>with a baton</u>. (The phrase modifies *motions*, telling how.)

A. Identifying Prepositional Phrases

Underline the prepositional phrases in the following sentences.

> EXAMPLE   There are few string instruments <u>in a band</u>.

1. Gustav Mahler's Symphony No. 3 is the longest of all symphonies.
2. Claude Monet painted hundreds of pictures of the same water-lily garden.
3. Among the most easily recognized photographs are those of Ansel Adams.
4. Julia Margaret Cameron, a pioneering photographer of the 19th century, developed new techniques in portrait photography.
5. During his career, Italian sculptor Giovanni Lorenzo Bernini worked for five popes.
6. Computer graphics can be used for research and entertainment.
7. Before the age of five, Wolfgang Amadeus Mozart had composed a concerto.
8. Between 1920 and 1937, George Gershwin wrote many songs with his brother.
9. Traditional folk dances originated within farming communities.
10. In the first decades of the 1900s, Russian ballerina Anna Pavlova was dancing throughout Europe, the Americas, and Asia.

B. Identifying Words Modified by Prepositional Phrases

Underline the prepositional phrase in each of the following sentences. Underline twice the word it modifies.

1. Many women on this reservation create silver jewelry.
2. During the winter months skiers can enjoy their sport.
3. The world's first books were made of clay and papyrus.
4. Benjamin Franklin founded the first hospital in the United States.
5. Scotland Yard is the headquarters of the London police force.
6. The game of football originated here.
7. The rhododendrons and the azaleas blossomed at the same time.
8. Behind the counter stood the worried clerk.
9. Some people call Magellan's voyage the greatest sailing feat in history.
10. These peppers come from Peru.

CHAPTER 3

Lesson 1

Prepositional Phrases

More Practice

A. Identifying Prepositional Phrases

Underline the prepositional phrase in each sentence. Write the word or words it modifies on the line.

1. Typhoid fever is caused by a bacterium that contaminates water and milk. _____

2. The star near the earth is the sun. _____

3. Take the patient to the nearest hospital. _____

4. Between the April showers we visited the park. _____

5. Our hockey team will play against your team tomorrow night. _____

6. The square dance is usually danced by four couples. _____

7. German bombs fell on England that year. _____

8. A syllogism is a form of reasoning. _____

9. In a syllogism, a major premise, or statement, and a minor premise are stated. _____

10. A logical conclusion is drawn from the two premises. _____

B. Identifying Prepositional Phrases as Modifiers

Underline the prepositional phrase in each sentence once. Underline the word or words it modifies twice. Then, in the blank, write **ADJ** or **ADV** to identify what kind of prepositional phrase it is.

> **EXAMPLE** Linda <u>will compete</u> <u>in a notable piano competition</u>. *ADV*

1. Early phonograph records of Enrico Caruso are valuable today. _____

2. Computer animation produces special effects for many films. _____

3. Frank Lloyd Wright turned against traditional architectural style. _____

4. Sculptures can be created from clay, wood, stone, plaster, or metal. _____

5. Artist Georgia O'Keeffe began painting the sky and clouds after an airplane ride. _____

6. Michelangelo created the ceiling frescoes in the Sistine Chapel. _____

7. The mobile sculpture was created by Alexander Calder. _____

8. The identity of the Mona Lisa is still a mystery. _____

9. Have you seen the movie about that concert pianist's life? _____

10. The woman behind the camera is Cindy Sherman, a photographer whose pictures feature herself. _____

For use with Pupil's Edition pp. 66–68

CHAPTER 3

Lesson 1 **Prepositional Phrases**   *Application*

A. Revising

Rewrite each sentence, changing the position of one or more prepositional phrases so that the sentence is no longer confusing. If there is no error, write **Correct.**

> **EXAMPLE** Jan borrowed a camera and took fine photos from her father.
> *Jan borrowed a camera from her father and took fine photos.*

1. The audience rewarded the actors with enthusiastic applause.

_____

2. That dancer does the highest jumps in the green costume.

_____

3. The young boy met the world-famous conductor at his first concert.

_____

4. My classmate taught a dance with red hair from Ireland.

_____

5. Tim designed the poster of the upcoming exhibit on the museum door.

_____

B. Using Prepositional Phrases as Modifiers

Revise each sentence below, adding one or more prepositional phrases to modify the words that are italicized. In parentheses after every prepositional phrase, write **ADJ** for adjective phrase or **ADV** for adverb phrase.

> **EXAMPLE** The *boy painted* a picture.
> *The boy at the table (ADJ) next to me (ADJ) painted a picture in only an hour (ADV).*

1. That *building* holds many *studios.*

_____

2. The artist *drew* a *sketch.*

_____

3. Artists *perfect* their skills.

_____

4. This artwork *is admired.*

_____

5. The artist's *paintings are displayed.*

_____

CHAPTER 3

Lesson 2

Appositives and Appositive Phrases

Reteaching

An **appositive** is a noun or pronoun that identifies or renames another noun or pronoun.

> Submersibles, <u>vessels</u> that operate under water, are used in research. (*Vessels* identifies *Submersibles*.)

An **appositive phrase** consists of an appositive plus its modifiers.

> Submersibles, <u>vessels that operate under water</u>, are used in research.

An **essential,** or **restrictive, appositive** defines the meaning of a noun or pronoun.

> The submersible <u>Alvin</u> can dive very deep. (*Alvin* identifies *submersible*.)

A **nonessential,** or **nonrestrictive appositive,** adds extra information about a noun or pronoun whose identity is already clear.

> Submersibles, <u>remarkable tools</u>, aid marine biologists.

A. Identifying Appositives and Appositive Phrases

Underline the appositive or appositive phrase in the following sentences.

1. Oceanography, the study of the ocean, often requires courage.
2. Many oceanographers work underwater at great depths, a dangerous environment.
3. Without supplies of the gas oxygen, humans cannot work for more than a few minutes below the surface of the water.
4. Tanks of compressed air, part of the equipment of scuba divers, enable these divers to go lower and stay longer underwater.
5. In 1715, English diver John Lethbridge used wood and leather to create the first diving suit.
6. The first safe device for underwater breathing, the aqua-lung, was invented in 1943.
7. Jacques-Yves Cousteau, a famous spokesperson for oceanographic research, was one of the inventors.

B. Identifying Essential and Nonessential Appositives

Underline the appositive or appositive phrase in each sentence below. On the line, identify each phrase as **E** if it is essential or **NE** if it is nonessential. Add necessary commas.

1. Swiss scientist Jacques Piccard is an oceanographic engineer.   _____

2. His father Auguste Piccard designed the bathyscaphe.   _____

3. In 1953, the two Piccards descended 10,300 feet under the Mediterranean Sea in the bathyscaphe *Trieste*.   _____

4. In 1960 Jacques and U.S. Navy officer Don Walsh took an even more dangerous ride in the *Trieste*.   _____

5. The scientists descended to 35,810 feet an incredible 6.8 miles below the surface of the Pacific Ocean.   _____

For use with Pupil's Edition pp. 69–70

Lesson 2 Appositives and Appositive Phrases

More Practice

A. Identifying Appositive Phrases

Underline the appositive phrase in each sentence. Write the noun it identifies on the line.

EXAMPLE The Pacific, <u>the largest ocean</u>, still holds mysteries. _____*Pacific*_____

1. The Great Barrier Reef, a chain of coral reefs, is located off the northeastern coast of Australia. _____

2. The ship *Endeavour* was under the control of Captain James Cook when it was badly damaged by the reef in the 18th century. _____

3. British explorer and navigator Matthew Flinders was the first to chart the coastline and navigate through an area of the reef. _____

4. The coral is formed by polyps, hardened skeletons of flowerlike water animals. _____

5. The coral formations, hundreds of species of living polyps attached to the coral, are a wide range of colors. _____

B. Using Appositives in Combining Sentences

Combine each pair of sentences by incorporating the information in the second sentence as an appositive in the first. Use commas if necessary.

1. Jacques Cousteau developed his lifelong passion while an officer with the French navy. Cousteau's passion in life was underwater exploration.

_____

2. Cousteau performed oceanic research on his ship. His ship was named *Calypso.*

_____

3. One of Cousteau's inventions was the diving saucer. The diving saucer is an underwater observation vehicle.

_____

4. Cousteau produced *The Undersea World of Jacques Cousteau. The Undersea World* was a television series about the drama of marine exploration.

_____

_____

5. In 1974, Jacques Cousteau began the Cousteau Society. The Cousteau Society is an organization that works to protect aquatic life.

_____

_____

CHAPTER 3

Appositives and Appositive Phrases

Application

A. Writing with Appositives and Appositive Phrases

Combine each set of sentences into a single sentence by using appositives or appositive phrases. Use commas as they are needed.

1. Jacques Cousteau was a marine explorer, writer, and filmmaker. He produced *The Silent World* (1953) and *World Without Sun* (1966). These films were both winners of Academy Awards.

_____

_____

2. *World Without Sun* is about five men living in an underwater capsule. This movie is a film documentary.

_____

_____

3. Exploring the floor of the ocean requires an underwater vehicle. The ocean floor still is a largely unmapped part of Earth.

_____

_____

4. Scientists have invented the bathyscaphe and other vehicles that can withstand water pressure well. Such underwater vehicles are called submersibles.

_____

_____

_____

B. Using Appositives and Appositive Phrases

You are an oceanographer who has just completed months of research on the waters off the coast of the United States. (Choose a coast.) Write a paragraph for the general public describing what you and your team did and learned. Use at least three appositives or appositive phrases in your paragraph. Underline the appositives and appositive phrases.

_____

_____

_____

_____

_____

_____

_____

For use with Pupil's Edition pp. 69–70

CHAPTER 3

Lesson 3 Verbals: Participles   *Reteaching*

A **verbal** is a verb form that acts as a noun, an adjective, or an adverb. A **participle** is a verbal that acts as an adjective; it modifies a noun or pronoun. Participles may be either present participles or past participles.

> <u>Gossiping</u>, she talked fast. (The present participle *gossiping* modifies *she*.)

> Please pick up the <u>dropped</u> coins. (The past participle *dropped* modifies *coins*.)

A **participial phrase** consists of a participle plus its modifiers and complements.

> <u>Gossiping with her friend</u>, she talked fast. (The participial phrase *Gossiping with her friend* modifies *she*.)

> Please pick up the coins <u>dropped by passersby</u>. (The participial phrase *dropped by passersby* modifies *coins*.)

A. Identifying Participles and Participial Phrases

In each sentence, find and underline a participle or participial phrase that modifies the boldfaced noun or pronoun. On the blank, write what kind of participle it is: **Present** for present participle or **Past** for past participle.

1. Writing quickly, the **students** took the exam.   _____

2. The travelers saw a huge stone **castle** perched on the rocky cliff.   _____

3. The **boy** performing a solo on the trumpet is my brother.   _____

4. Swimming with a friend, **Frances** made it to the float.   _____

5. The stolen **briefcase** contained valuable documents.   _____

6. Ed's **sailboat,** damaged near the stern, was unusable.   _____

7. I couldn't open the box with the **hinges** rusted shut.   _____

8. The Statue of Liberty shows a **woman** holding a lighted torch.   _____

B. Identifying Participles and Participial Phrases

Underline the participle or participial phrase in each sentence. Underline twice the word that the participle or participial phrase modifies.

1. The refusal to obey laws one considers unjust is called civil disobedience.

2. Susan B. Anthony, arrested for voting, was struggling for women's rights.

3. Objecting to the Mexican War, the writer Henry David Thoreau refused to pay a tax.

4. A night spent in jail was his penalty.

5. Thoreau wrote an essay, "Civil Disobedience," inspired by this incident.

6. Consistently opposing violence, the Dalai Lama promotes peaceful methods in his quest for independence of his homeland, Tibet.

CHAPTER 3

Lesson 3

Verbals: Participles

More Practice

A. Identifying Participles and Participial Phrases

Underline once the participle or participial phrase in each sentence. Underline twice the word that the participle or participial phrase modifies. On the blank, write what kind of participle it is: **Present** for present participle and **Past** for past participle.

1. Living in South Africa in 1893, Mohandas K. Gandhi, an Indian, experienced racism. _____

2. He took up the cause of all maligned nonwhites. _____

3. Returning to India, he decided to work for his country's independence from Britain. _____

4. Influenced by his Hindu beliefs, Gandhi felt that violence was wrong. _____

5. Sensing support from his people, he worked to promote nonviolent change. _____

6. Risking arrest, he disobeyed laws that he considered unfair. _____

7. As he appealed to the conscience of a disturbed populace, this man hoped for an end to racial injustice. _____

8. Employing nonviolent means, Gandhi helped India to achieve independence. _____

9. This inspired leader was called "Mahatma," which means "Great Soul." _____

10. Gandhi died violently, assassinated by a political extremist. _____

B. Using Participial Phrases to Combine Sentences

Use participial phrases to combine each set of sentences into one sentence.

EXAMPLE The tiger watched its prey intently. The tiger prepared to strike.
Watching its prey intently, the tiger prepared to strike.

1. The soccer players were exhausted. They collapsed on the grass.

_____

2. The Grand Canyon is located in Arizona. The Grand Canyon is a spectacular sight.

_____

3. The library needed money for new books. The library sponsored a craft fair.

_____

4. The hurricane swept up the coast. It destroyed everything in its path.

_____

5. The tourists relaxed on the beach. They were enjoying their visit to Miami.

_____

For use with Pupil's Edition pp. 71–72

Lesson 3

Verbals: Participles

Application

A. Using Participial Phrases to Combine Sentences

Combine each of these pairs of sentences as a single sentence by using participial phrases. Use a comma after each participial phrase that begins a sentence.

1. Many workers joined the National Farm Workers Association. The organization was founded by Cesar Chavez.

_____

_____

2. Chavez headed a workers' struggle. The struggle was supported by organized labor, religious groups, and students.

_____

_____

3. Chavez had worked as a migrant farm worker. Because of this experience, he became aware of farm workers' problems early in life.

_____

_____

B. Using Participles and Participial Phrases in Writing

On the blank to the right of each participle or participial phrase below, write what kind of participle it is: **Present** for present participle and **Past** for past participle. Then write a sentence using the participle or phrase. Use a comma after each participial phrase that begins a sentence. Underline the words the participles and participial phrases modify.

1. laughing _____

_____

2. searching for the treasure _____

_____

3. painted on the wall _____

_____

4. displayed in the museum _____

_____

CHAPTER 3

Lesson 4

Verbals: Gerunds

Reteaching

A **gerund** is a verbal that ends in *–ing* and acts as a noun. A **gerund phrase** consists of a gerund plus its modifiers and complements.

> This summer I will take a course on <u>using the bow and arrow</u>.
>   GERUND   GERUND PHRASE

In sentences, gerunds and gerund phrases may be used anywhere nouns may be used.

Function	Example
As subject	**<u>Using</u> the bow and arrow** made William Tell famous.
As predicate nominative	My goal is **<u>becoming</u> a competent archer**.
As direct object	The teacher demonstrates **<u>holding</u> the bow correctly**.
As object of a preposition	Daily practice helps in **<u>developing</u> archery skills**.
As indirect object	I wanted to give **<u>using</u> the bow and arrow** a chance.

A. Identifying Gerunds and Gerund Phrases

In each sentence, underline every gerund phrase once. Underline each gerund twice.

1. Skiing is an extremely popular sport in many countries.
2. The sport consists of gliding over snow on runners called skis.
3. Speeding down mountain slopes thrills many skiers.
4. *Cross-country style* identifies hiking on skis over snow-covered ground.
5. Norwegian immigrants introduced skiing into the United States in the mid-1800s.
6. Many fans enjoy watching ski competitions.
7. Almost every ski area in the United States has machines for making snow.
8. Ski areas also have ski lifts, devices for transporting skiers to the tops of slopes.

B. Identifying Gerunds and Gerund Phrases

Underline each gerund or gerund phrase. On the blank, write how it is used: **S** for subject, **PN** for predicate nominative, **DO** for direct object, **OP** for object of a preposition, or **IO** for indirect object.

1. Playing paddle tennis is a new sport for me. _____

2. A doubles game, paddle tennis requires practicing. _____

3. Playing with perforated wooden rackets is a strange sensation. _____

4. My tennis strategy of hitting the ball hard did not work in this game. _____

5. After retrieving the soft rubber ball, I had to learn to lob it. _____

6. Now our winter enjoyment is playing paddle tennis. _____

7. First, of course, we must complete shoveling the snow off the court. _____

8. If the ball goes over the fence, our dog finds it by sniffing it out. _____

9. One problem in winter is getting enough exercise. _____

10. Athletes can stay in shape by playing paddle tennis. _____

For use with Pupil's Edition pp. 73–74

CHAPTER 3

Lesson 4

Verbals: Gerunds

More Practice

A. Identifying Gerunds and Gerund Phrases

Underline each gerund or gerund phrase. In the blank, write how it is used: **S** for subject, **PN** for predicate nominative, **DO** for direct object, or **OP** for object of a preposition.

1. Many people enjoy playing on sports teams. _____

2. Others prefer participating in sports individually. _____

3. Skateboarding is an individual sport that began in California in the early 1960s. _____

4. This activity requires balancing skillfully on a short board on wheels. _____

5. One of the oldest sports in the United States is surfing, a skill from Hawaii. _____

6. Many adventurers are attracted to the challenge of scaling difficult slopes. _____

7. Swimming laps is a popular form of recreation and is great exercise. _____

8. Another sport swimmers may enjoy is diving from high boards. _____

9. Fencing was one of the original sports to be included in the modern Olympics. _____

10. Before participating in a race, runners should train thoroughly. _____

B. Using Gerunds and Gerund Phrases

Use gerund phrases to combine each set of sentences into one sentence.

1. His goal became an obsession. He wanted to run a four-minute mile.

   _____

2. Frank liked many activities in shop class. He especially liked to work with the jigsaw.

   _____

3. Nancy received recognition from her fellow designers. The experience gave her more confidence.

   _____

4. He wore green every St. Patrick's Day. Doing so reminded him of his Irish heritage.

   _____

5. Can you hear the waves? They are pounding on the rocks.

   _____

CHAPTER 3

Lesson 4

Verbals: Gerunds

Application

A. Using Gerunds and Gerund Phrases

Write sentences using the following gerunds and gerund phrases in the sentence parts indicated in parentheses.

1. in-line skating (subject) _____

_____

2. gliding on the ice (object of preposition) _____

_____

3. carrying a backpack (predicate nominative) _____

_____

4. canoeing down a river (direct object) _____

_____

5. competing in a gymnastics event (your choice of position) _____

_____

B. Using Gerunds and Gerund Phrases in Writing

You are the publicist for an indoor sports facility. Some activities and equipment available at the facility are listed below. Choose one of the items and write a paragraph about it for the facility's advertising brochure. Make using the equipment or joining in the activity at this facility sound appealing. Use five or more gerunds in your statement.

weight lifting   mechanical rowing machines   rock climbing wall
racquetball   stair climbing machines   water exercises

_____

_____

_____

_____

_____

_____

_____

_____

For use with Pupil's Edition pp. 73–74

CHAPTER 3

Lesson 5 Verbals: Infinitives   *Reteaching*

An **infinitive** is a verbal that usually begins with the word *to* and acts as a noun, an adjective, or an adverb. In each example below, the infinitive is *to find*. An **infinitive phrase** consists of an infinitive plus its complements and modifiers.

As noun   <u>To find the lost child</u> was everyone's goal. (subject of sentence)
                   We all wanted <u>to find the lost child</u>. (direct object)
                   Our goal was <u>to find the lost child</u>. (predicate nominative)

As adverb   <u>To find the lost child</u>, we combed the woods. (*To find the lost child* modifies *combed*, telling why.)

As adjective   Our efforts <u>to find the lost child</u> ended in success. (*To find the lost child* modifies *efforts*.)

A. Identifying Infinitives and Infinitive Phrases

Underline the infinitive phrase in each sentence. Underline twice the infinitive.

EXAMPLE How long will it take <u><u>to walk</u> to Chester Library</u>?

1. The tourists asked the bus driver to go slower.
2. Their purpose for taking the tour was to see the countryside.
3. The earliest attempts to fly ended in embarrassment, if not injury.
4. Robert's plan to compete in a triathlon surprised everyone.
5. In the spring, crabs begin to shed their shells.
6. I gave up chocolate to lose weight.
7. To fulfill a lifelong dream, Dad bought a small boat.
8. The coach's decision to quit surprised everyone.
9. The audience wanted the guitarist to play another tune.
10. To help his school's publication, he joined the newspaper staff.

B. Identifying Infinitive Phrases

Underline the infinitive phrase in each sentence. On the blank, write how it is used:
N for noun, **ADJ** for adjective, or **ADV** for adverb.

1. For his job, Janine's father needed to do research in Spain for a year.   _____

2. However, to leave the family that long would be difficult.   _____

3. The family met to decide the best course of action.   _____

4. Everyone in the family decided to spend a year in Madrid.   _____

5. Now they are all working to study a new language.   _____

6. "My ambition is to speak like a native Spaniard," Janine's brother proclaimed.   _____

7. "I hope Spanish is not too hard to master," replied Janine.   _____

8. The decision to live abroad makes her a little nervous as well as excited.   _____

Lesson 5

Verbals: Infinitives

More Practice

A. Identifying Infinitive Phrases

Underline the infinitive phrase in each sentence. On the blank, write how it is used:
N for noun, **ADJ** for adjective, or **ADV** for adverb.

1. The landlord expects to paint the apartment next month. _____

2. We made an attempt to lift the log off him. _____

3. Ginny moved quickly to stop the running child. _____

4. To be a soccer goalie requires unwavering concentration. _____

5. Charles Dickens wrote novels to make money. _____

6. The shoes to buy are the most comfortable pair. _____

7. In fall the ptarmigan begins to shed its brown feathers for winter white. _____

8. The insurance company promised to repay everyone affected by the flood. _____

9. To keep your scholarship, you must maintain a high grade-point average. _____

10. Yes, we packed supplies—enough to last a full week. _____

11. The ant's ability to carry comparatively huge weights impressed the child. _____

12. His prize was to be invited into the press box during the playoff games. _____

B. Using Infinitive Phrases

Use each of the following infinitive phrases in a sentence.

1. to claim your luggage

_____

2. to avoid slipping

_____

3. to make enough money

_____

4. to hear the ocean

_____

5. to get your signature

_____

For use with Pupil's Edition pp. 75–77

Lesson 5

Verbals: Infinitives

Application

A. Using Infinitive Phrases to Combine Sentences

Combine each pair of sentences below, changing one of the sentences into an infinitive phrase. Add, drop, or change words as needed.

EXAMPLE The library board hired an architect. He will design a new building.
REVISION *The library board hired an architect to design a new building.*

1. The spy plane flies low. That way it avoids showing up on radar.

_____

2. Ted will get up very early tomorrow. That is what he expects.

_____

3. Anita found the right costume. She will wear it to the Halloween party.

_____

4. The dog barked loudly. Its action frightened the intruder.

_____

5. Ludwig lost an important ability. He could no longer hear his own music.

_____

B. Using Infinitive Phrases for Variety

Listening to a speaker, you took notes in sentences that are almost all short and in the same pattern. Now you want to use your notes in writing a report with a variety of sentence patterns. Combine ideas in these notes in a paragraph of five or six sentences. (You need not include all the ideas.) Use infinitive phrases in at least three of the sentences.

Languages change over time. People speaking a certain language move to different places. The different groups start speaking a little differently. Each group starts using new words. The groups may change the way they say the sounds in the words. In time, the groups are speaking different languages. Some linguists study how languages change and grow. They compare words in different languages that name the same things. Similar words suggest shared roots. The linguists can figure out family trees of languages.

_____

_____

_____

_____

_____

_____

_____

Lesson 6

Placement of Phrases

Reteaching

If a writer places a phrase in the wrong position in a sentence, the sentence can become confusing or take on a wrong meaning. A **misplaced phrase** is a phrase that is placed so far from the word it modifies that the meaning of the sentence is unclear or incorrect.

EXAMPLE The volcano destroyed the town erupting suddenly.
(Did the town erupt?)

REVISION Erupting suddenly, the volcano destroyed the town.

A **dangling phrase** is a phrase that is intended to modify a word that does not appear in the sentence.

EXAMPLE Erupting suddenly, the villagers were terrified. (The villagers were not erupting.)

REVISION Erupting suddenly, the volcano terrified the villagers.

A. Finding the Words Modified by Misplaced Phrases

Each underlined phrase is misplaced. On the line to the right, write the word that the phrase was intended to modify.

1. We saw a video of Mr. Hayward's trip to Alaska <u>in our geography class</u>.

_____

2. <u>To get ice cream</u>, don't forget your promise.

_____

3. You can see the Statue of Liberty <u>flying into Kennedy Airport</u>.

_____

4. <u>Covered with mustard and relish</u>, I fully enjoyed the sausage.

_____

5. We witnessed an accident <u>on the way to our school</u>.

_____

6. The schoolchildren saw the train <u>looking out the window</u>.

_____

B. Identifying Misplaced Phrases and Dangling Modifiers

Underline the misplaced phrase or dangling modifier in each of the following sentences. Then rewrite the sentence, correcting the error. Add or change words as needed.

1. Stepping on the gas, the car lurched forward.

_____

2. Suspected of espionage, the FBI arrested the two brothers.

_____

3. Having escaped from his captors, freedom was finally achieved.

_____

4. I watched the deer run across the meadow with my mother.

_____

5. The school to upgrade computer equipment received a grant.

_____

For use with Pupil's Edition pp. 78–79

Placement of Phrases

More Practice

Correcting Misplaced Phrases and Dangling Modifiers

If a sentence contains a misplaced phrase or dangling modifier, rewrite it to eliminate the error. If the sentence is correct, write **Correct.**

1. Eating under the porch, I saw a squirrel.

_____

2. Using many time- and labor-saving devices, the project was finally finished.

_____

3. Above my head, I heard the jet.

_____

4. Ignoring table manners, contestants in the pie-eating contest gobbled up the pies.

_____

5. Adjusting the floodlights, the stage was now fully lighted.

_____

6. The streetcar is fondly remembered by many people gently swaying and quietly clicking down the track.

_____

_____

7. Once almost totally abandoned, many cities are now resurrecting their trolley lines.

_____

8. Rushing to get ready for school, the phone rang.

_____

9. The rooms were cleaned by the custodians without any students inside them.

_____

10. Walking down the street, the flowers in the neighbor's yard looked beautiful.

_____

11. Left alone in the house, he was terrified by the thunderstorm.

_____

12. My foot missed a step, carrying the heavy box up the stairs.

_____

13. Running through the rain, his clothes became wet.

_____

14. At only eight years of age, my father took me to my first baseball game.

_____

Placement of Phrases

Application

A. Correcting Misplaced Phrases and Dangling Modifiers

If a sentence contains a misplaced phrase or dangling modifier, rewrite it to eliminate the error. If the sentence is correct, write **Correct.**

1. Sprinting for all he was worth, the record was broken by the runner.

   _____

2. The puppies abandoned next to the roadside were placed in good homes.

   _____

3. After singing the national anthem, the game started.

   _____

4. Children stopped to pick some apples running through the orchard.

   _____

5. To reach the shelf, the stepladder was used.

   _____

B. Correcting Misplaced Phrases and Dangling Modifiers in Writing

Rewrite this paragraph, correcting any misplaced phrases or dangling modifiers.

     Sir George Cayley invented the first successful glider, but he was not the first to fly in it. Having designed and flown several experimental models, Cayley's coachman was chosen to be the first glider pilot. The coachman was persuaded to get into the glider at the top of the hill with soothing words. Once inside the glider, Cayley gave the machine a hard shove. Rolling down the hill at perhaps 25 miles an hour, Cayley watched the machine take off. It landed safely several hundred feet away, but its occupant was not happy. Getting out of the glider, Cayley saw him trembling. The coachman immediately quit his job catching his breath. "I was hired to drive, not to fly!" he exclaimed.

_____
_____
_____
_____
_____
_____
_____
_____
_____
_____
_____

For use with Pupil's Edition pp. 78–79

Lesson 7

Sentence Diagramming: Phrases

More Practice 1

A. Prepositional Phrases

Adjective Phrases

The fifteenth child of Josiah Franklin was a man of many talents.

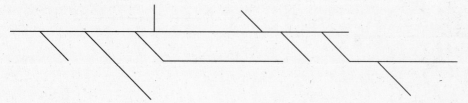

Adverb Phrases Benjamin Franklin left his mark on history.

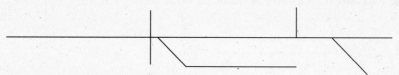

B. Appositive Phrases

Franklin, a runaway apprentice at 17, eventually became a prominent citizen.

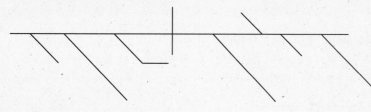

C. Participial Phrases

Taken out of school at ten, Franklin studied composition, science, mathematics, and languages on his own.

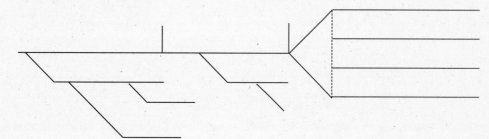

CHAPTER 3

Lesson 7

Sentence Diagramming: Phrases

More Practice 2

D. Gerund Phrases

His master (an older brother) resented Ben's writing unsigned articles for the paper.

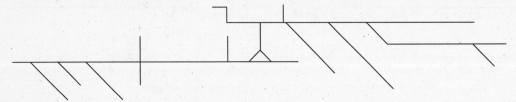

E. Infinitive Phrases

Infinitive Phrase as Noun The headstrong apprentice determined to leave his unappreciative master.

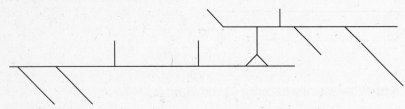

Infinitive Phrase as Modifier His decision to go to Philadelphia was a fortunate choice.

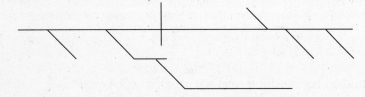

For use with Pupil's Edition pp. 80–83

CHAPTER 3

Lesson 7

Sentence Diagramming: Phrases

Application

On a separate piece of paper, diagram each of the following sentences.

A. Diagramming Prepositional, Appositive, and Participial Phrases

1. Philadelphia, the largest city in the American colonies, offered many opportunities for an eager worker.
2. Within seven years, Franklin owned his own print shop.
3. In 1730 he married Deborah Read, the daughter of his first Philadelphia landlady.
4. For 25 years he published an almanac called *Poor Richard's Almanac*.

B. Diagramming Gerund Phrases and Infinitive Phrases

1. Publishing a newspaper and an almanac did not fill Franklin's time.
2. He also liked to do scientific experiments.
3. One of his interests was learning about electricity.
4. In his experiments, he barely avoided electrocuting himself.

C. Mixed Practice

1. Inventing useful devices came naturally to him.
2. A civic leader, he saved lives by introducing the first fire department.
3. As deputy postmaster for all the colonies, he improved mail delivery.
4. In the 1750s, Franklin was one of the first leaders to propose a union of the colonies.
5. Later, he was elected to serve in the Continental Congress.
6. He advised Thomas Jefferson in writing the Declaration of Independence.
7. Serving as ambassador to France, Franklin convinced the French to support the American cause.
8. To find another person with Franklin's abilities would be virtually impossible.

CHAPTER 3

Lesson 1

Kinds of Clauses

Reteaching

A **clause** is a group of words that contains both a subject and a verb.
An **independent,** or **main, clause** expresses a complete thought and
forms a sentence.

> My favorite <u>season</u> <u>is</u> spring.
> **SUBJECT   VERB**

A **subordinate,** or **dependent, clause** contains a subject and a verb but does not
express a complete thought and cannot stand alone as a sentence. Subordinate
clauses are often introduced by such words as *although, if, because, how, what,
why, that, when,* and *since.*

> **Although the days are cool** (What happens despite this?)

A subordinate clause must always be combined with an independent clause.

> <u>Although the days are cool,</u> <u>the sun is visible longer.</u>
> **SUBORDINATE CLAUSE   INDEPENDENT CLAUSE**

A subordinate clause should not be confused with a verbal phrase, which does not
have a subject and a verb.

> <u>Tracking hours of sunlight,</u> we look forward to summer.   (phrase)

> <u>As we track hours of sunlight,</u> we look forward to summer. (subordinate clause)

A. Identifying Clauses

Identify each boldfaced group of words by writing **C** for a clause and
P for a phrase.

1. The seasons occur **because the amount of sunlight changes.**   _____

2. **With the days so short and the sun so low in the sky,** the winter air
barely warms up.   _____

3. Spring nights are usually cool, **but spring days may be warm.**   _____

4. **Hanging high in the sky,** the sun heats up summer days.   _____

B. Identifying Independent and Subordinate Clauses

Identify each boldfaced group of words by writing **IND** for independent clause
or **SUB** for subordinate clause.

1. A full moon appears larger **as it emerges from behind clouds.**   _____

2. **The housefly has five eyes,** which are located on the upper part of its head.   _____

3. **While red lights repel birds,** white lights attract them.   _____

4. The campers learned **what the poison ivy vine looks like.**   _____

5. **What bedtime story will you tell the children** if they stay up late?   _____

6. When Peter changed his clothes for the party, **he forgot to comb his hair.**   _____

For use with Pupil's Edition pp. 92–94

CHAPTER 4

Lesson 1

Kinds of Clauses

More Practice

A. Identifying Phrases and Independent and Subordinate Clauses

Identify each boldfaced group of words by writing **P** for a phrase, **IC** for an independent clause, and **SC** for a subordinate clause.

1. **After Anthony worked all summer as a waiter,** he bought a car. _____

2. The king issued a proclamation **against shooting bears in the region.** _____

3. **When the sun is close to the horizon,** it looks larger. _____

4. Since Cleo moved to New York six months ago, **she has had three jobs.** _____

5. **There were no newspapers in America** until one was published in Boston in 1690. _____

6. **Climbing the stairs to the top of the Washington Monument** requires endurance. _____

7. The person **who is climbing the hill** is my mother. _____

8. **If you have solved that puzzle,** I'll give you a more difficult one. _____

9. **After making several comparisons,** Greg was ready to buy a stereo. _____

10. When Katrina arrived home after the late band practice, **she was tired.** _____

B. Identifying Independent and Subordinate Clauses

Each sentence contains two clauses. In the blanks provided, identify each clause as independent or subordinate by writing **IND + IND, IND + SUB,** or **SUB + IND.**

1. Weather forecasts are of interest to all of us, but they are vital to pilots, sailors, and farmers. _____

2. Because knowledge of the weather is so important, forecasters take great care to be accurate. _____

3. Forecasters take measurements from weather stations, which are located all over the world. _____

4. Did you know that the Eureka weather station is only 600 miles from the North Pole? _____

5. Satellites transmit weather data, and computers assemble the information. _____

6. When it was launched on April 1, 1960, *Tiros I* was the first weather satellite. _____

7. Since weather high up in the atmosphere affects weather below, forecasters send up balloons carrying instruments. _____

8. Small parachutes carry the instruments down until they are safely on the ground. _____

CHAPTER 4

Kinds of Clauses

Lesson 1

Application

A. Using Subordinate Clauses in Writing

Rewrite each sentence, adding a subordinate clause that begins with the word in parentheses.

> **EXAMPLE** The customer requested a TV. (that)
> *The customer requested a TV that would fit on a desk.*

1. My mother does not approve of my watching TV. (unless)

_____

2. We were just sitting down to dinner. (when)

_____

3. French is the language. (that)

_____

4. We will win the championship. (if)

_____

5. George Washington was commander-in-chief of the Continental Army. (before)

_____

_____

B. Revising

The following paragraph has no capitalization to mark sentence beginnings, or end marks to indicate their endings. Insert a period after the last word of each sentence, and mark the first letter in each sentence with a triple underscore ≡, the proofreading symbol for capitalization. When you are finished, write the number of sentences that combine both an independent and a dependent clause.

Number of sentences with both an independent and a dependent clause: _____

Before weather forecasters used satellites and radar, people looked for clues in nature for predicting the weather since people did not have sophisticated equipment, they watched the behavior of animals, birds, and insects some signs are reliable, but others should not be trusted here are some examples of what people once believed if you can see a groundhog's shadow on February 2, there will be six more weeks of winter when the sky is red at sunset, good weather will follow when the sky is red at sunrise, the weather can't be trusted Germans kept frogs to predict rain because frogs croak more in low air pressure pinecones have been used to forecast weather because they open up in dry weather they close up when the weather is damp we are lucky that weather forecasting techniques have improved.

For use with Pupil's Edition pp. 92–94

CHAPTER 4

Adjective and Adverb Clauses

Reteaching

An **adjective clause** is a subordinate clause that is used as an adjective to modify a noun or pronoun. Like adjectives, adjective clauses answer the questions *which one*, *what kind*, *how much*, or *how many*. They are introduced by a **relative pronoun** (such as *that, who, whom, whose,* and *which*) or a **relative adverb** (such as *when, where,* and *why*).

> The White House, <u>where every president since 1800 has lived</u>, is our most famous residence. (*Where* is the White House?)

> John Adams was the president <u>who first lived there</u>. (*Which* president?)

An **essential,** or **restrictive, clause** provides information that is necessary to identify the preceding noun or pronoun. A **nonessential,** or **nonrestrictive, clause** provides additional, but not necessary, information about a noun or pronoun in a sentence where the meaning is already clear. Use commas to set off a nonessential clause.

> A structure <u>that honors our first president</u> is the Washington Monument. (essential)

> The monument, <u>which stands 555 feet tall</u>, is an imposing landmark. (nonessential)

When choosing between *that* and *which*, use *that* to introduce essential clauses and *which* to introduce nonessential clauses.

An **adverb clause** is a subordinate clause that is used as an adverb to modify a verb, adjective, or adverb.

> I visit the United States Capitol <u>whenever I am in Washington, D.C.</u> (*When* do I visit? Modifies verb.)

> The building is more impressive <u>than I imagined</u>. (*How* impressive? Modifies adjective.)

Adverb clauses are usually introduced by **subordinating conjunctions** such as these:

after	because	if	than	until	where
although	before	since	though	when	wherever
as	even though	so	unless	whenever	while

Identifying Adjective and Adverb Clauses

Underline once the adjective or adverb clause. Underline twice the word it modifies.

1. The poet T.S. Eliot, who was born in the United States, became a British subject.
2. After Bob arrived in Madrid, he began to study art.
3. The person whose name heads the list had to drop out of the race.
4. Ed gave the package to his father, who will mail it tomorrow.
5. Mountain gorillas, which are an endangered species, live only in Africa.
6. Before the snow began, we stacked two cords of firewood.
7. The man whom you met is the theater manager.
8. Because that clerk was so helpful, I praised her to the store manager.
9. The cross-country team is curious about the course that it will run.
10. Children should use car safety seats until they are four years old.

CHAPTER 4

Adjective and Adverb Clauses

More Practice

A. Identifying Adjective and Adverb Clauses and Introductory Words

In each sentence, underline the adjective or adverb clause once. Underline the word modified twice. On the line, write the relative pronoun or relative adverb that introduces the adjective clause or the subordinating conjunction that introduces the adverb clause.

> **EXAMPLE** Throw the <u>fruit</u> <u>that spoiled</u> into the compost heap.   *that*

1. Lesotho is an African country that is surrounded by another country. _____

2. I read "The Secret Sharer" by Joseph Conrad, who was born in Poland. _____

3. The movie was beginning as George bought our tickets. _____

4. What was the date when Neil Armstrong stepped on the moon? _____

5. Whenever you make a promise, you must keep it! _____

6. You may keep the pot of gold if you answer three questions correctly. _____

7. Hawaii is a state that is made up of several islands. _____

8. The music that you heard was composed by our group. _____

9. Marlene can skate better than many professional skaters can. _____

10. Something that always bothers me is a large crowd. _____

B. Identifying Essential Clauses

Underline the adjective clause in each of the following sentences. Write **ESS** on the line to the right if the clause is an essential adjective clause. Write **NON** if it is a nonessential clause. Insert commas where they are needed.

1. The Galapagos Islands are known as the place where giant tortoises are found. _____

2. The legend about this waterfall is one that has never been authenticated. _____

3. Beaver tail which I have never tried is regarded as a delicacy. _____

4. May gave the key to her mother who opened the door. _____

5. The winner of the essay contest that I entered will be announced today. _____

6. Cans, shoes, and clothing are among the things that goats will nibble. _____

7. A man who lived in this town sailed his little boat across the Atlantic. _____

8. The llama which is a member of the camel family is found in South America. _____

9. Marla called the girls she had selected for the team. _____

10. Those friends usually meet at a storefront cafe where the food is cheap. _____

For use with Pupil's Edition pp. 95–97

Lesson 2

Adjective and Adverb Clauses

Application

A. Using Essential and Nonessential Clauses in Writing

Combine each numbered pair of sentences to form one sentence containing an adjective clause that modifies the boldfaced word. If the clause is nonessential, add commas. If the clause is essential, do not add commas.

1. Ms. Lopez is a coach. She is always fair and helpful.

_____

2. I have seen that **movie** five times. That is my favorite movie.

_____

3. The **city** is growing rapidly. I visited the city last summer.

_____

4. I read a book about **Albert Einstein.** He was a brilliant scientist.

_____

5. The **Big Dipper** can help you find your way at night. It is a constellation with seven stars.

_____

_____

B. Using Adjective and Adverb Clauses

Rewrite each of the following sentences, adding an adjective or adverb clause that begins with the word in parentheses. Set off with commas any adverb clause that comes at the beginning or the middle of the sentence, and any nonessential adjective clause.

1. The boys ran into the building. (Use *where.*)

_____

2. I've already searched for an hour! (Use *where.*)

_____

3. The book has finally been returned to the library. (Use *that.*)

_____

4. The squirrel ran up the tree. (Use *which.*)

_____

5. The squirrel ran up the tree. (Use *before.*)

_____

6. Nobody may enter this room. (Use *after.*)

_____

_____

CHAPTER 4

Noun Clauses

Reteaching

A **noun clause** is a subordinate clause that is used as a noun. A noun clause may be used anywhere in a sentence that a noun can be used.

Subject	**What occurred on January 24, 1848,** changed California.
Direct Object	James W. Marshall discovered **that there was gold there.**
Indirect Object	The gold brought **whoever craved it** great adventure.
Predicate Nominative	Quick fortunes were **what the forty-niners sought.**
Object of a Preposition	Their futures depended on **how lucky they were.**

Usually, a noun clause is introduced by one of these words: a **subordinating conjunction,** such as *that, how, when, where, whether,* and *why;* or a **relative pronoun,** such as *what, whatever, who, whom, whoever, whomever, which,* and *whichever.* A pronoun that introduces a clause has no antecedent in the sentence. With or without an introductory word, if you can substitute the word *someone* or *something* for a clause in the sentence, it is a noun clause.

A. Identifying Noun Clauses

In each sentence, underline the noun clause used as the sentence part identified in parentheses.

1. Whether this area was visited by French explorers is what I've been wondering about for years. (predicate nominative)

2. I've been telling whoever will listen that I once found a strange coin near French Creek. (indirect object)

3. What appears to be French is printed on whatever surface is legible. (object of a preposition)

4. Whomever I asked couldn't explain how the coin came to be in this area. (subject)

5. From what the book says, I learned that French explorers were here. (direct object)

6. Now what I'm wondering is why their explorations here are not better known. (subject)

B. Identifying Noun Clauses and Their Uses

Underline the noun clause in each sentence. Then, on the line, indicate how the noun clause is used: write **S** for subject, **DO** for direct object, **IO** for indirect object, **PN** for predicate nominative, or **OP** for object of a preposition.

1. No one knows who invented the wheel. _____

2. My favorite time of year is when the leaves change color. _____

3. The store's delivery service will give priority to whoever calls first. _____

4. That the moon affects the tides is a scientific fact. _____

5. The glare of the sun was what affected the infielder's performance. _____

6. Did you understand what Darryl was saying? _____

For use with Pupil's Edition pp. 98–100

Lesson 3

Noun Clauses

More Practice

A. Identifying Noun Clauses and Their Uses

Underline the noun clause in each sentence. Then, on the line, indicate how the noun clause is used: write **S** for subject, **DO** for direct object, **IO** for indirect object, **PN** for predicate nominative, or **OP** for object of a preposition.

1. Wherever the baby stays for ten minutes becomes crowded with
admiring relatives.   _____

2. I've forgotten whose poems I was supposed to study tonight.   _____

3. This guidebook is what you need for your backpacking tour of Europe. _____

4. The journalists described how the survivors lived.   _____

5. The classified ads will show you where you can find a job.   _____

6. Whoever wins the primary election will run in the general election this fall. _____

7. This explanation of how the videotape recorder works is not at all clear! _____

8. That Socrates believed in democracy is questionable.   _____

9. There is no excuse for what happened today.   _____

10. The committee will award whoever comes in first a special cup.   _____

B. Using Noun Clauses

Write sentences using the following noun clauses as indicated in parentheses.

> **EXAMPLE** what is in the box (subject)
> *What is in the box is a mystery.*

1. why the experiment failed (direct object)_____

_____

2. whichever candidate gets the most votes (object of preposition) _____

_____

3. what every coach wants (predicate nominative) _____

_____

4. whoever comes to the door (indirect object) _____

_____

5. that you have seen the same things before (subject) _____

_____

CHAPTER 4

Lesson 3 # Noun Clauses

Application

A. Using Noun Clauses

Rewrite each numbered sentence by including a noun clause used as shown in parentheses. Replace the word or phrase that is currently serving that role in the sentence. Underline the noun clause in each new sentence.

(1) A New Yorker is accustomed to heavy traffic and crowded streets. **(subject) (2)** However, the traffic may give a visitor a shock. **(indirect object) (3)** I remember my first visit to the city. **(direct object) (4)** The plays on Broadway were my goal. **(predicate nominative) (5)** However, the noise made me want to return to my hometown. **(object of preposition)**

1. _____

2. _____

3. _____

4. _____

5. _____

B. Writing with Noun Clauses

Imagine you are writing an article for the local newspaper about the history of your town. Create an interesting character or event that could have happened sometime in your town's past, and write about it for the paper. In your article, include at least five sentences using noun clauses. Show at least three of the possible uses of noun clauses: subject, direct object, indirect object, predicate nominative, and object of preposition. Use a separate piece of paper if necessary.

_____

_____

_____

_____

_____

_____

_____

_____

_____

_____

For use with Pupil's Edition pp. 98–100

Sentence Structure

Lesson 4

Reteaching

A sentence's structure is determined by the number and kind of clauses it contains. A **simple sentence** has one independent clause and no subordinate clauses. Any part of the sentence, such as subject or verb, may be compound.

> The Panama Canal connects the <u>Atlantic</u> and <u>Pacific Oceans</u>. (compound object)

A **compound sentence** has two or more independent clauses joined together. Any of the following can be used to join independent clauses: a comma with a coordinating conjunction; a semicolon; or a semicolon with a conjunctive adverb and a comma.

> <u>The Panama Canal connects the Atlantic and Pacific Oceans</u>; <u>it took more than ten years to build</u>. (two independent clauses joined together by a semicolon)

A **complex sentence** has one independent clause and one or more subordinate clauses.

> The Panama Canal, <u>which took more than ten years to build</u>, was opened in 1914.
> SUBORDINATE CLAUSE

A **compound-complex sentence** has two or more independent clauses and one or more subordinate clauses.

> The Panama Canal, <u>which took more than ten years to build</u>, was opened in 1914, **but** it received little attention because of the outbreak of World War I.

Identifying Kinds of Sentences

Identify each sentence with **S** for simple, **CD** for compound, **CX** for complex, or **CC** for compound-complex.

1. On December 7, 1941, Japanese planes took off from aircraft carriers; hours later they attacked Pearl Harbor in Hawaii. _____

2. Congress declared war on Japan the next day. _____

3. American involvement in World War II, which lasted four years, affected almost every American family. _____

4. The government instituted a program, which was called rationing, that limited how much of certain items civilians could buy. _____

5. In 1942, the United States Navy sank four Japanese aircraft carriers; moreover, the United States Army Air Force joined Britain in a bombing campaign. _____

6. The D-Day invasion, which was the largest seaborne invasion in history, occurred on June 6, 1944; it led to Germany's ultimate defeat. _____

7. Franklin Delano Roosevelt had led the country since 1933. _____

8. Although Roosevelt's health was failing, he ran for president a fourth time in 1944, and he won. _____

9. Everything was going well for the country; however, President Roosevelt died suddenly on April 12, 1945. _____

10. World War II, which the United States had played a big part in winning, finally ended on September 2, 1945; consequently, the United States emerged as a leading world power. _____

CHAPTER 4

Sentence Structure
More Practice

A. Identifying Kinds of Sentences

Identify each sentence below with **S** for simple, **CD** for compound, **CX** for complex, or **CC** for compound-complex.

1. After they defeated Germany in World War II, the Allies divided Germany and its capital city, Berlin, into four sectors: a British sector, a French sector, an American sector, and a Russian sector. _____

2. The British, French, and American sectors became the Federal Republic of Germany. _____

3. The Russian sector became the German Democratic Republic, or East Germany, and Berlin was in that sector. _____

4. The East Germans tried to make Berlin their capital, but ultimately they could only have East Berlin because the Americans, French, and British controlled West Berlin. _____

5. East Germans who tried to cross the border to West Germany were prevented from doing so by East German border guards, mines, and barbed wire. _____

6. Many East Germans escaped to the West by taking the subway from East Berlin to West Berlin; from West Berlin they could reach other western cities. _____

7. Because so many people escaped, East Germany did not have enough workers, and the East German government erected a wall between East Berlin and West Berlin. _____

8. In 1989, the Berlin Wall finally came down; the two Germanys were united the following year. _____

B. Building Sentences

Build sentences by adding words, phrases, and clauses to the simple sentence below. Keep the structures from the preceding sentences in each new sentence.

That child plays.

1. Add an adjective and an object to the sentence. _____

_____

2. Now add an adverb and a prepositional phrase. _____

_____

3. Add another independent clause. _____

_____

4. Add a subordinate clause. _____

_____

For use with Pupil's Edition pp. 101–103

Lesson 4

Sentence Structure

Application

A. Using Different Structures to Combine Sentences

The following paragraph consists entirely of simple sentences. Give the paragraph variety by combining some of the sentences to form compound, complex, and/or compound-complex sentences. Write the revised paragraph on the lines below. In parentheses after each sentence, label the sentence type.

> After World War II, relations between the United States and the Soviet Union deteriorated. They reached the most dangerous point in October, 1962. The Russians had secretly installed nuclear missiles in Cuba. Cuba is located less than 100 miles from Florida. President Kennedy ordered a naval blockade. He threatened the Soviet Union. He said the United States would stop any Soviet ship trying to bring weapons to Cuba. The world faced the threat of nuclear war. This lasted about a week. Then Premier Khrushchev of the Soviet Union backed down. He ordered the removal of missiles from Cuba.

_____

_____

_____

_____

_____

_____

_____

_____

B. Using Different Sentence Structures

Write a paragraph about an event in recent history that concerns the national government—a new law or tax bill from Congress, an appointment by the president, or a treaty or other action on the international scene. Include at least one of each kind of sentence: simple, compound, complex, and compound-complex. In parentheses after each sentence, label the sentence type. Use a separate piece of paper if necessary.

_____

_____

_____

_____

CHAPTER 4

Sentence Diagramming

More Practice 1

Complete each diagram with the sentence provided.

A. Simple Sentences

All of us have used street maps.

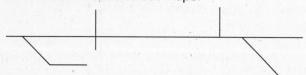

B. Compound Sentences

A street map may be the most typical kind of map, but it is only one of many.

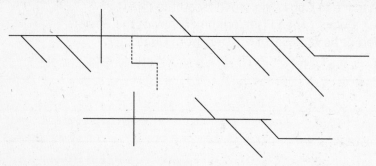

C. Complex Sentences

Adjective Clause Introduced by a Pronoun

An inventory map is one that shows the location of special land features.

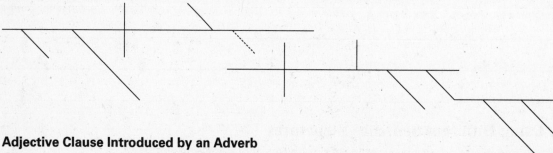

Adjective Clause Introduced by an Adverb

On your map, mark in dark green the places where forests are found.

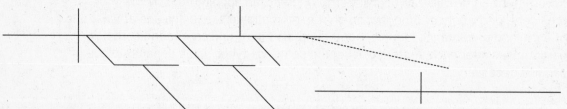

Adverb Clause

Before maps can be drawn, someone must survey the land.

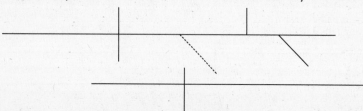

For use with Pupil's Edition pp. 104–107

Copyright © McDougal Littell Inc.

Lesson 5 — Sentence Diagramming

More Practice 2

C. Complex Sentences *(continued)*

Noun Clause Used as Subject

How map makers obtain data has improved greatly in recent years.

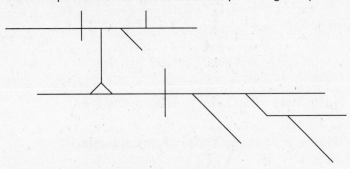

Noun Clause Used as Direct Object

Aerial photos clearly show where mountains, rivers, and other natural features lie.

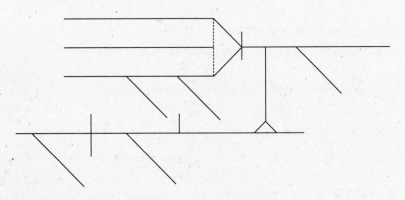

D. Compound-Complex Sentences

Whoever makes a map today depends on computers, and we who use the maps appreciate their accuracy.

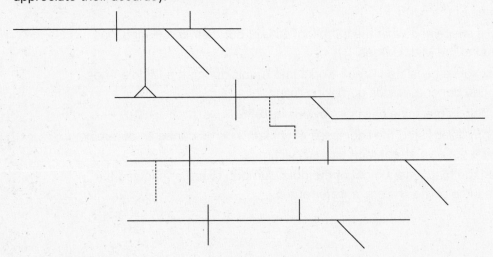

CHAPTER 4

Sentence Diagramming

Application

On a separate piece of paper, diagram each of the following sentences.

A. Diagramming Simple Sentences, Compound Sentences, and Complex Sentences

1. We use several kinds of mobility maps, which guide people from one place to another place.

2. Often transit maps showing the routes of buses and subways use diagrams called *schematics*.

3. Road maps show different kinds of roads with different kinds of lines, and they include scales indicating distances.

4. Before anyone sets a course for a ship, he or she must consult nautical charts of the area.

B. Diagramming Complex Sentences and Compound-Complex Sentences

1. Airplane pilots must know where mountains and tall structures are.

2. A street map is similar to a road map, but it focuses on a smaller area, which is shown in greater detail.

3. Whoever is curious about the location of countries should consult an atlas.

4. Where the political boundaries of countries lie is shown on general reference maps, and these maps are updated frequently.

C. Mixed Practice

1. The oldest map that is still in existence is from Babylonia.

2. It was the Babylonians who introduced the system of dividing a circle into 360 degrees, and their idea led to lines of longitude and latitude on maps.

3. In classical Greece, the mathematician Eratosthenes calculated the circumference of the earth.

4. Many Greeks suspected what the earth looked like, but their knowledge was forgotten during the Middle Ages.

5. After Arab scholars translated Greek works into Arabic during the Middle Ages, they developed better methods of making maps.

6. How maps help in medicine became obvious in 1855.

7. An English physician listed the addresses of cholera victims during an outbreak, and he drew a dot on a street map for each victim.

8. The place on the map where most of the dots clumped together showed the doctor the source of the cholera, a water pump.

For use with Pupil's Edition pp. 104–107

Lesson 1

Sentence Fragments

Reteaching

A **sentence fragment** is a part of a sentence that is punctuated as if it were a complete sentence. A sentence must have at least one subject and one verb, and must express a complete thought. To correct a fragment, add the missing part. Or, if the fragment is in a paragraph, join it with the complete sentence before it. Watch for these types of fragments.

Freestanding subject or verb Some fragments lack a subject or a verb.

Fragment   Our planet.
Correction   Our planet is called Earth.

Subordinate clauses as fragments A subordinate clause has a subject and a verb, but it does not express a complete thought.

Fragment   Before Galileo lived.
Correction   Before Galileo lived, people called Earth the center of the universe.

Phrases as fragments A phrase is a group of words with neither a subject nor a verb. Some kinds of phrases are prepositional, infinitive, and participial.

Fragment   Defying accepted beliefs. (participial phrase)
Correction   Defying accepted beliefs, Galileo presented a new view.

Others Watch for parts of a compound predicate or items in a series written as sentences.

Fragments   And learned about other objects. Asteroids, meteoroids, and comets.
Correction   Astronomers studied the skies and learned about other objects: asteroids, meteoroids, and comets.

Recognizing Fragments

If the group of words is a sentence, write **S** on the line. If it is a fragment, write **F.**

1. Since 1600, telescopes have used lenses or mirrors to gather and focus light.   _____

2. Going outside the earth's atmosphere to see more clearly.   _____

3. The surface temperature of the sun is 8,700 degrees Fahrenheit.   _____

4. Estimated 100 billion galaxies in our universe.   _____

5. The stars in the Milky Way, including our sun.   _____

6. To study the night sky throughout the year.   _____

7. Many stargazers use telescopes on their roof porches.   _____

8. When people thought that the sky was an upside-down blue bowl over the earth.   _____

9. The planets closest to the sun are Mercury, Venus, Earth, and Mars.   _____

10. To find a logical explanation for the movements of stars.   _____

CHAPTER 5

Lesson 1

Sentence Fragments

More Practice

A. Identifying Fragments and Their Missing Parts

If the group of words is a sentence, write **S** on the line. If it is a fragment, write **F**.

1. Constellations, small groups of stars.   _____

2. Orion, Andromeda, Cassiopeia, and hundreds of others.   _____

3. From early times, people gave names to constellations.   _____

4. In a yearly orbit, passing through 12 constellations called the zodiac. _____

5. Told stories about the stars.   _____

6. When they saw the moon change shape.   _____

7. For instance, Andromeda, the character in a Greek myth.   _____

8. Stars seem to twinkle.   _____

B. Correcting Sentence Fragments

Use each fragment below in a complete sentence. Write your sentence on the line.

1. Looking for the constellation Orion.

_____

2. The first sign of the zodiac Aquarius, the Water Bearer.

_____

3. To find the Big Dipper on a clear night.

_____

4. Studying the heavens for information about the stars.

_____

5. If you go outside with a telescope on an August night.

_____

_____

6. Too far away to be seen.

_____

7. Stars such as white dwarfs, novae, supernovae, quasars, and pulsars.

_____

_____

For use with Pupil's Edition pp. 116–119

CHAPTER 5

Lesson 1

Sentence Fragments

Application

A. Correcting Sentence Fragments Within a Paragraph

Rewrite each of the numbered pairs of word groups to eliminate the fragments. Change punctuation and capitalization and delete or add words as necessary.

(1) Facts about the earth are impressive. If you take the time to think about them. (2) Did you know that all magnets point north? Because the earth itself is a giant magnet. (3) Dinosaur bones tell tales. About life on earth 65 million years ago. (4) Higher levels of carbon dioxide in the atmosphere raise global temperatures. And produce the greenhouse effect. (5) Studies of the ocean also reveal surprises. Undersea mountain ranges, hot vents, and spreading of the sea floor.

1. _____

_____

2. _____

_____

_____

3. _____

_____

4. _____

_____

5. _____

_____

B. Recognizing and Revising Sentence Fragments

Find the sentence fragments in the following hastily written paragraph. On the lines below, write the number of each fragment. Then write it as a complete sentence, either by combining it with the previous sentence or by adding the missing parts. Use a separate piece of paper if necessary.

(1) In 1957, *Sputnik*, a Russian satellite, was the first to orbit Earth. (2) Since then many countries more than 100 satellites. (3) In 1960, the United States sent up the first weather satellite. (4) Named *Tiros I*. (5) Other satellites, including *Ranger VII*, *Pioneer 10*, and *Pioneer 11*, studied the moon, Jupiter, and Saturn. (6) And radioed back important information. (7) In 1961, Russia and the United States began sending humans into space. (8) With Russia again taking the lead. (9) The United States was determined to be first on the moon. (10) In 1969, U.S. astronauts made the first moon landing in *Apollo 11*.

_____

_____

_____

_____

CHAPTER 5

Lesson 2

Run-On Sentences

Reteaching

A **run-on sentence** is two or more complete sentences incorrectly written as one. Run-ons are formed when a writer incorrectly uses only a comma between sentences (called a **comma splice**) or joins two sentences without any punctuation at all.

> Outdoor concerts are held every summer, they attract all ages.

You can correct a run-on by separating the two sentences.

> Outdoor concerts are held every summer. They attract all ages.

It may also be possible to join them correctly in one of these ways:

1. Add a comma and a conjunction such as *and, but, or*, and *for*.

> Outdoor concerts are held every summer, and they attract all ages.

2. Add a semicolon.

> Outdoor concerts are held every summer; they attract all ages.

3. Add a semicolon and a conjunctive adverb such as *however, therefore*, and *thus*.

> Outdoor concerts are held every summer; moreover, they attract all ages.

A. Identifying Run-On Sentences

Identify each sentence as either **Run-on** or **Correct**.

1. In several large cities the orchestras give their summer performances in outdoor settings, the Cleveland Orchestra, for example, plays at Blossom Music Center. _____

2. The Chicago Symphony Orchestra plays at Ravinia Park north of the city during the summer, and the Grant Park Symphony Orchestra plays in the city itself. _____

3. The Boston Pops Orchestra gives outdoor concerts in a park on the Charles River these concerts are free. _____

4. Outdoor music settings are not used only by the orchestras; on the contrary, all types of music are presented during the season. _____

5. During a single weekend a stage might be used by an orchestra, a rock band, and a jazz combo, audiences have a choice. _____

6. Often summer orchestra programs end with fireworks displays this is especially true on holiday weekends such as the Fourth of July. _____

B. Correcting Run-On Sentences

In each run-on below, draw a vertical line between words to show where the first idea ends.

1. Outdoor music settings are very informal consequently, many people like them.

2. You can go early with a picnic basket the concert area might have a restaurant and food stands, too.

3. People spread out blankets, eat, and talk, later they lie on the blankets to listen to the music.

4. Parents take young children the children can move around during the program.

For use with Pupil's Edition pp. 120–121

Lesson 2

Run-On Sentences

More Practice

A. Recognizing and Correcting Run-On Sentences

Correct any run-on sentence below, either by separating it into two sentences or combining the sentences correctly. Write the corrected sentence or sentences on the line(s). If the sentence is correct as is, write **Correct.**

1. Can you name three kinds of music, most people at least know classical music.

_____

_____

2. Rock music once had half of all music sales since the mid-80s its popularity has dropped.

_____

_____

3. Jazz sales have remained steady, they have consistently held to about 3.5 percent of

recorded music sales. _____

_____

4. Taking only 3.8 percent of music sales in 1987, rap grew to 9 percent of sales by 1999.

_____

_____

5. Cassettes were the best-selling music format in the 1980s, today CDs are preferred by

most consumers. _____

_____

B. Correcting Sentence Run-Ons

Rewrite the paragraph below, correcting any run-on sentences.

Why have compact discs become so popular, they cost almost twice as much as albums and cassettes. It is because discs hold a large amount of music, furthermore, CD players can be programmed to selective choice. The CD revolution has revived the music industry. Teenagers are still the largest consumers of recorded music adult buying is up.

_____

_____

_____

_____

_____

CHAPTER 5

Lesson 2 Run-On Sentences

Application

A. Identifying Sentence Fragments and Run-Ons

Determine which word groups in this paragraph are correct sentences, fragments, or run-ons. Write the number of each group on the correct line below.

(1) Most European nations took centuries to adapt. **(2)** To recent medical, industrial, and technological changes. **(3)** Korea is typical of countries that modernized in less than a century. **(4)** For almost 2,000 years. **(5)** Its population remained around ten million. **(6)** Since 1930, it has increased 700 percent, why? **(7)** Surrounded by water. **(8)** In earlier times, the peninsula gave up many of its men to the sea, today, safe seagoing vessels have made seafaring a less dangerous occupation. **(9)** And have also increased opportunities for commercial fishing. **(10)** Antibiotics have reduced life-threatening diseases, better medical knowledge and enlightened sanitation practices have lowered infant deaths.

1. Complete sentences: _____

2. Fragments: _____

3. Run-ons: _____

B. Rewriting to Eliminate Run-On Sentences

Rewrite the following paragraph on world population trends to eliminate run-on sentences.

The world is gaining more people, its population is projected to pass six billion by 2025 some think it will surpass eight billion in mid-century. Most of the growth is likely to take place in developing countries, Europe, it is thought, will reduce its numbers from 500 million to 486 million by the first quarter of the century. Africa's population will continue to be the fastest growing, it tripled between 1950 and 1990. Some think it will reach two-and-one-quarter billion in 2050, showing a 1,000 percent increase it will then contain almost one-fourth of the world's inhabitants.

_____

_____

_____

_____

_____

_____

_____

_____

For use with Pupil's Edition pp. 120–121

CHAPTER 5

Lesson 1 — The Principal Parts of a Verb *Reteaching*

Every verb has four principal parts: the present, the present participle, the past, and the past participle. The principal parts are used to make all of a verb's tenses and other forms.

The past and past participle of a **regular verb** are formed by adding *–ed* or *–d* to the present. Most verbs are regular. However, spelling changes are needed in some words, for example, *bury-buried*.

We **work** hard. (Present)   We are **working** together. (Present participle)
We **worked** yesterday. (Past)   We have **worked** all week. (Past participle)

The past and past participle of an **irregular verb** are formed some way other than adding *-ed* or *-d* to the present. Here are some examples:

	Present	Past	Past Participle		Present	Past	Past Participle
Group 1 Forms of the Present, Past, & Past Participle are same	burst	burst	(has) burst	**Group 4** Past Participle formed by adding *-n* or *-en* or the Past	beat	beat	(have) beaten
	cut	cut	(has) cut		bite	bit	(have) bitten
	hurt	hurt	(has) hurt		break	broke	(have) broken
	let	let	(has) let		lie	lay	(have) lain
	put	put	(has) put		tear	tore	(have) torn
Group 2 Forms of Past & Past Participle are same	bring	brought	(has) brought	**Group 5** Past Participle formed from Present—adding *-n* or *-en*	draw	drew	(have) drawn
	catch	caught	(has) caught		eat	ate	(have) eaten
	lay	laid	(has) laid		give	gave	(have) given
	lend	lent	(has) lent		go	went	(have) gone
	swing	swung	(has) swung		grow	grew	(have) grown
Group 3 Vowel changes from *i* to *a* to *u*	begin	began	(has) begun		rise	rose	(have) risen
	drink	drank	(has) drunk		see	saw	(have) seen
	ring	rang	(has) rung		throw	threw	(have) thrown
	sink	sank	(has) sunk		write	wrote	(have) written
	swim	swam	(has) swum				

Using the Principal Parts of Verbs

Complete each sentence by adding the correct form of the verb given in parentheses.

1. Nancy has _____ the flu from her sister. (catch)

2. My dog is _____ regular dog food now; last month he _____ puppy food. (eat)

3. My best friend has _____ across the lake several times. (swim)

4. The custodian informed us that the water pipes had _____. (burst)

5. I hope you have not _____ your promise. (break)

6. Earlier, Dad _____ the newspaper on the table. (lay)

CHAPTER 6

Lesson 1

The Principal Parts of a Verb

More Practice

A. Writing the Correct Forms of Verbs

Decide which form of each verb given in parentheses is needed: the past or the past participle. Write the correct form on the line.

> **EXAMPLE** The boat had (sink) before help arrived. ___*sunk*___

1. The sweater has (shrink) in the dryer. _____

2. I haven't (speak) to my cousin since last summer. _____

3. We (wear) our most comfortable clothes for the long flight. _____

4. Pam (bite) into the juicy pear. _____

5. José (lie) down on the sofa after the five-mile hike. _____

6. The price of gas has (rise) in the last few weeks. _____

7. Marty (see) the "Help Wanted" sign in the shop window and applied for the job. _____

8. Mrs. Sullivan has (teach) at our school for 20 years. _____

9. The Pied Piper (lead) the children out of Hamelin. _____

10. Many flowers (grow) despite the cold weather. _____

B. Using the Correct Forms of Verbs

Underline the correct verb form of the two in parentheses. Write **P** or **PP** to identify whether the part of the verb you chose is the past or the past participle.

> **EXAMPLE** At the seventh-inning stretch, the audience (raised, <u>rose</u>). ___*P*___

1. The new bridge has (cost, costed) the city a great deal of money. _____

2. Have the speakers (brang, brought) along any audiovisuals? _____

3. The foolish sun-worshippers have (laid, lain) out in the sun for hours. _____

4. Reneé has (swam, swum) farther than she ever did before. _____

5. Corey (swang, swung) at the first pitch. _____

6. I (saw, seen) the expression on her face. _____

7. My ankle (hurt, hurted) severely when I broke it. _____

8. The slacks (shrank, shrunk) from the heat in the dryer. _____

9. We have (drank, drunk) a whole gallon of lemonade this afternoon. _____

10. The baby cried when her balloon (burst, bursted). _____

For use with Pupil's Edition pp. 130–133

CHAPTER 6

Lesson 1 # The Principal Parts of a Verb   *Application*

A. Proofreading for the Correct Forms of Verbs

Draw a line through each incorrect verb form in this paragraph. Draw this proofreading symbol ∧ next to the error and, in the spaces between lines of type, write the correct form of the verb.

EXAMPLE *Have you b̶r̶i̶n̶g̶e̶d̶ ∧ any photographs of your trip to the West?* (brought)

We saw many varieties of cactuses as we travel through the deserts of Tucson. I was amazed to see that all of these different kinds of cactuses— crown of thorns, rosette succulents, prickly pear, and saguaro—growed side by side. On our second day in Tucson, we gone to visit the Arizona-Sonora Desert Museum. Some of the best exhibits we seen were dioramas of Arizona wildlife. All afternoon I study how real the animals and plants looked in the displays. In one diorama, coyotes howled at a full moon. In another, a roadrunner runned across the fields. The day ended too quickly; however, I writed postcards to all my friends while the sights of the Desert Museum were still fresh in my mind. We just wished that we had went to Kitt Peak National Observatory, too.

B. Using Principal Parts Correctly

List the principal parts of each word below. Then write a paragraph that uses at least five of the verb parts, and underline each one. Make sure all verb forms are used correctly.

1. lose _____
2. bring _____
3. bite _____
4. rise _____
5. shine _____
6. spring _____

_____
_____
_____
_____
_____
_____
_____

Copyright © McDougal Littell Inc.

CHAPTER 6

Verb Tense

Lesson 2

Reteaching

A **tense** is a verb form that shows the time of an action or condition. These tenses are used to indicate whether an action or condition is in the past, the present, or the future, and to indicate how events are related in time. Tenses are formed from the principal parts. Notice below that the verb form doesn't change between singular and plural except in present and present perfect.

Simple Tenses:	*Singular*	*Plural*
Present	I/you wave	we/you wave
	he/she/it waves	they wave

This tense shows that an action or condition is occurring in the present, or occurs regularly, or is constantly or generally true.

Past	he/she/it waved	they waved

This tense shows that an action or condition occurred in the past.

Future	he/she/it will wave	they will wave

This tense shows that an action or condition will occur in the future.

Perfect Tenses:	*Singular*	*Plural*
Present Perfect	I/you have waved	we/you have waved
	he/she/it has waved	they have waved

This tense shows that an action or condition was completed at one or more indefinite times in the past, or began in the past and continues in the present.

Past Perfect	he/she/it had waved	they had waved

This tense shows that an action or condition in the past preceded another past action or state.

Future Perfect	he/she/it will have waved	they will have waved

This tense shows that an action or condition in the future will precede another future action or condition.

A. Identifying Verb Tenses

Underline the verb in each sentence and write its tense on the blank.

1. Shawn bought a new watch recently. _____

2. By tomorrow, he will have owned the new watch for a whole week. _____

3. Shawn had kept his old watch from the sixth grade. _____

4. Manufacturers have introduced added features on watches. _____

5. My watch, for instance, shows time in three different time zones. _____

B. Using Verb Tenses

Underline the better tense of the verb in parentheses.

1. Ray (practices, practiced) this song every day for the past week.

2. We made sure that the pond (freezes, had frozen) before we went skating.

3. Nick always (gives, had given) his young brother a head start when they race.

4. Alice (drove, will drive) us home from the basketball game tomorrow.

5. Roger (has wondered, will wonder) about that ever since it happened.

For use with Pupil's Edition pp. 134–137

CHAPTER 6

Lesson 2 Verb Tense

More Practice

A. Using Verb Tenses

On the line, write the verb in parentheses in the tense indicated.

1. Once the blockers (past perfect of *create*) a hole, Dan plunged through it. _____

2. Today (present of *promise*) to be a great day for fishing. _____

3. The press (past of *applaud*) respectfully as the mayor entered the room. _____

4. "Tomorrow we (future of *experiment*) with sulfuric acid," said Ms. Ames. _____

5. We (present perfect of *grow*) tomatoes in this plot for the last ten years. _____

6. At this rate, Al (future perfect of *break*) two track records by year's end. _____

7. "That rookie (future of *swing*) at anything," muttered the coach. _____

8. Before she ran for mayor, Ms. Jordan (past perfect of *garner*) much support. _____

9. By the end of December, Isaiah (future perfect of *earn*) $4,000. _____

10. Many older people (present perfect of *have*) difficulty using a computer. _____

B. Correcting Verb Tenses

Decide whether each underscored verb is in the correct tense. If it is correct, do nothing. If it is in the wrong tense, draw a line through it. Then draw this proofreading symbol ∧ next to the word and write the correct tense above the error.

EXAMPLE The word *clock* ~~will come~~ *came* from the French word *cloche*, which means "bell."

The clocks of today <u>look</u> nothing like the first mechanical clocks. The first clocks had no display of numerals, either digital or on a traditional round face. In those "clocks," gears, chains, and weights <u>are</u> connected to one or more bells. As the weight <u>has fallen</u>, it moved the gears. When the gears <u>will have turned</u> to a certain position, they set the bells into motion. Hearing the bells, people knew another hour <u>has passed</u> since the last time the bells <u>will ring</u>. Inventors of the 1200s <u>have developed</u> the earliest mechanical clocks. The people of that era <u>appreciated</u> the convenience. Who wouldn't? Sundials do not work at night or on cloudy days. Hourglasses and water clocks <u>will be</u> hard to use. The earliest mechanical clocks were not very reliable. However, inventors improved them gradually. By the mid-1700s, the mechanical clock <u>had reached</u> its final form.

CHAPTER 6

Verb Tense

Application

A. Identifying and Using Verb Tenses

Underline the verb in each sentence and write the tense above it. Then, on the line, write the verb in the tense indicated in parentheses.

> **EXAMPLE** George <u>had admitted</u> his earlier mistakes. (past)   *admitted*
> *past perfect*

1. The polyorchis jellyfish looked like an electric light bulb. (present) _____

2. By today the climbers will reach the summit. (future perfect) _____

3. New Zealand is the leading producer of kiwi fruit.
   (present perfect) _____

4. Jake played lacrosse for two years. (past perfect) _____

5. My great-grandmother turns 100 years old this May. (future) _____

6. The famous pirate, William Kidd, was once an honest sea
   captain. (past perfect) _____

B. Using Verb Tenses

Recall what you know about timepieces of all kinds, from sundials through mechanical clocks and digital watches to atomic timepieces. Use each of the following verbs in a sentence on the topic of measuring time. Use the verb tense indicated in parentheses.

1. improve (past) _____

   _____

2. avoid (present perfect) _____

   _____

3. invent (past perfect) _____

   _____

4. count (future perfect) _____

   _____

5. use (present) _____

   _____

6. adapt (future) _____

   _____

For use with Pupil's Edition pp. 134–137

Progressive and Emphatic Forms

Reteaching

The **progressive form** of a verb expresses an event in progress. Each of the six tenses has a progressive form, made by using the same tense of the verb *be* with the present participle.

These tenses show action in progress at a given time.	These tenses show action that begins and is in progress before another action occurs in that time.
Present progressive is jumping	**Present perfect progressive** has been jumping
Past progressive was jumping	**Past perfect progressive** had been jumping
Future progressive will be jumping	**Future perfect progressive** will have been jumping

The **emphatic form** of a verb gives special force to the verb. It is used only in the present and past tenses. It is commonly used to correct or contradict.

Present   I do jump. He does jump.   **Past**   She did jump. They did jump.

Identifying Progressive and Emphatic Verb Forms

Underline the verb in each of these sentences. Then, on the line, identify the verb's form, using these abbreviations: **pres. prog., past prog., fut. prog., pres. perf. prog., past perf. prog., fut. perf. prog., pres. emph.,** and **past emph.**

1. Lola has been practicing with her new drum set. _____

2. Nguyen will be judging the arts show with me. _____

3. The choir is singing at the folk festival in May. _____

4. I did follow all of the instructions on the package! _____

5. The squirrels in the backyard really do chase each other over the birdhouse. _____

6. The three girls were deciding on a route for their bike trip. _____

7. My sister had been taking tennis lessons before her accident. _____

8. It will be snowing by this time tomorrow afternoon. _____

9. Ricardo did hear you. _____

10. They will have been living in Ashland for 20 years this June. _____

11. Is your cousin in England following any particular team this year? _____

12. The twins really did eat four ice cream cones yesterday. _____

13. The theater will be installing a new sound system next month. _____

14. The mayor does understand the need for better recreational facilities. _____

15. Has your pet frog been hiding under the bed again? _____

CHAPTER 6

Lesson 3

Progressive and Emphatic Forms

More Practice

A. Using Progressive and Emphatic Verb Forms

On the line, write the verb in parentheses in the form indicated.

1. Descendants of the *Bounty* mutineers (present perfect progressive of *live*) on Pitcairn Island since the 18th century. _____

2. The actress (present progressive of *appear*) in the road company of the play. _____

3. Alpha Centauri (present emphatic of *shine*) more brightly than many other stars. _____

4. Cheryl and I (past perfect progressive of *plan*) to ask the teacher about the assignment. _____

5. By Thanksgiving, Janine (future perfect progressive of *work*) in the customer service department for three years. _____

6. A secret British computer (past perfect progressive of *break*) German codes for two years when the first U.S. electronic computer went into operation in 1945. _____

7. The candidate (present emphatic of *intend*) to visit every state in the Union. _____

8. Until his fall, Eliot (past perfect progressive of *beat*) his own record in the 100-meter race. _____

9. When you are in class, I (future progressive of *sleep*) on the other side of the globe. _____

10. Lloyd (past emphatic of *score*) the highest in the class on the last test. _____

B. Using Correct Verb Forms

Write the progressive or emphatic form of the verb given, using the correct tense.

1. As she does research for her history paper, Zora (discover) interesting facts about our

   nation's history. _____

2. For example, although she (hear) the name Sacagawea before, she never really knew

   what Sacagawea did. _____

3. Zora learned that Sacagawea (live) in what is now North Dakota before the explorers

   Meriwether Lewis and William Clark arrived. _____

4. The Shoshone woman joined the expedition, and in time she (translate) for the explorers

   as they met with different tribes. _____

5. Zora hopes that she (find) more facts about Sacagawea soon. _____

6. She (plan) to spend a good deal of time in the library doing research. _____

For use with Pupil's Edition pp. 138–139

Progressive and Emphatic Forms

Application

Identify progressive or emphatic forms that can be substituted for the underlined verbs to improve the paragraph. Write the forms you choose on the lines below.

The family that **(1)** has lived next door for the last four years has a ten-year-old boy. Last summer he always **(2)** got into trouble. I **(3)** believe that he was not bad; the problem was he had nothing to do. Then his grandmother went into an assisted-living apartment. She **(4)** had fallen often and no longer wanted to live alone. I remember the first time Kevin told me, "I **(5)** will visit my grandmother this weekend." When he came back from the visit, he reported, "Grandma and three of her friends in the building **(6)** have problems with their VCRs and remotes. I wasn't there long, but I **(7)** fixed Grandma's VCR today. Next weekend I'll go back and help some of Grandma's friends." Each time Kevin was at the building, other residents asked for his help. By the end of this month, my neighbor **(8)** will have volunteered his services at the senior citizens building for six months. The residents of the building **(9)** will throw a party in his honor. Lately I **(10)** have wondered where I can volunteer.

1. _____   6. _____

2. _____   7. _____

3. _____   8. _____

4. _____   9. _____

5. _____   10. _____

B. Using Verb Tenses

Choose any six of these verbs. Use progressive or emphatic forms of the six chosen verbs, plus additional verbs in any form you need, in a paragraph about a team project you have worked on. The project could be for school, on a job, or for fun. Underline the chosen verbs where they appear in the paragraph.

plan	manage	select	supervise	begin
continue	complete	do	correct	assist
improve	analyze	encourage	frustrate	

_____

_____

_____

_____

_____

_____

_____

CHAPTER 6

The Voice of a Verb

Reteaching

The voice of an action verb indicates whether the subject **performs** or **receives** the action. When a verb's subject *performs* the action expressed by the verb, the verb is in the **active voice.** Most of the sentences you write will be in the active voice.

> For centuries, the river **carved** the rocks. (The subject *river* performs the action.)

When a verb's subject *receives* the action expressed by the verb, the verb is in the **passive voice.** A passive voice verb is formed by combining a form of the verb *be* with the past participle of the main verb. The passive voice is often used when the person or thing performing the action is indefinite or unknown.

> The rocks **were carved** by the river. (The subject *rocks* receives the action.)

Identifying Active and Passive Voice

In each sentence, underline the complete verb with a single line. If the performer of the action is identified, underline that word twice. Decide whether the verb is in active voice (the subject is the performer) or passive voice (the subject is not the performer). On the line at the right, label each sentence with **A** for active voice or **P** for passive voice.

Example The generators <u>are powered</u> by the <u><u>waterfall</u></u>. ___*P*___

1. John Philip Sousa wrote "The Stars and Stripes Forever." _____

2. Fruit crops in Florida were destroyed by the cold weather. _____

3. This food was donated by schoolchildren. _____

4. The stars have always fascinated people. _____

5. An award was presented to the museum's governing board. _____

6. The elephant is the only animal with four knees. _____

7. Several antique cars were owned by the eccentric millionaire. _____

8. Only the fastest animals survived the forest fire. _____

9. The fire was started by lightning. _____

10. Snow at the top of the tallest mountains never melts. _____

11. These narrow inlets along the shore are called *fiords*. _____

12. When was Mount Everest first conquered? _____

13. Iron spikes may be attached to the soles of hiking boots
    for a good grip on ice or snow. _____

14. How fast does a glacier move? _____

15. The highest navigable lake in the world is found on the border between
    Bolivia and Peru. _____

For use with Pupil's Edition pp. 141–142

The Voice of a Verb

More Practice

A. Identifying Active and Passive Voice Verbs

Underline the complete verb in each of the following sentences. On the line to the right, label the verbs in active voice **A** and the verbs in passive voice **P**.

1. The noon whistle announced lunchtime. _____

2. A shadow was cast on the day by Jennifer's uncooperative attitude. _____

3. A fire engine clanged down the boulevard. _____

4. That poem describes city sounds of all kinds. _____

5. Was the poem written by an American poet? _____

6. Hawaiians have used surfboards for more than 100 years. _____

7. That ball has been hit out of the park! _____

8. The windows were installed by a local company. _____

9. Nothing prepares a traveler for the poverty of this city. _____

10. The official rainfall for the area is measured at the airport. _____

B. Using Active and Passive Voice Verbs

Write each verb in parentheses using the correct tense and the correct voice.

1. Four of the five Great Lakes (share) by Canada
and the United States. _____

2. The Great Lakes (hold) almost one-fifth of the fresh surface
water in the world. _____

3. The lakes (dig) by slowly moving glaciers over
25,000 years ago. _____

4. Before the glaciers melted, they (move) numerous times across
what is now the Great Lakes area. _____

5. Today, the water in Lake Erie (drop) 326 feet, 99 meters,
to Lake Ontario. _____

6. The Great Lakes (consider) by some to be deep pools
connected by narrow channels. _____

7. Before 1900, all the water in the Great Lakes (drain) into
the St. Lawrence River. _____

8. With the opening of the Chicago Sanitary and Ship Canal in
1900, the course of the Chicago River was changed, and since
then its water (flow) away from Lake Michigan. _____

9. Inland ports like Chicago, Cleveland, and Buffalo (connect) to
the Atlantic Ocean by the St. Lawrence Seaway. _____

Lesson 4

The Voice of a Verb

Application

A. Revising to Avoid Passive Voice

You can make the following description of the Hubbard Glacier more lively by changing the verbs that are in passive voice to the active voice. On the lines below, rewrite the numbered sentences in the active voice. Add words where necessary. Use a separate piece of paper if needed.

The Hubbard Glacier is grinding to a stop at the head of the Yakutat Bay. **(1)** The mouth of the bay is being closed by the glacier. **(2)** Animals inside the bay are being trapped by the ice flow. **(3)** When the glacier moves, a roaring sound is heard by people. The trapped water is gushing out. **(4)** Ice and debris are carried away by the water. **(5)** On some occasions, the waves from the rushing water are estimated by onlookers to be 30 feet high.

1. _____

2. _____

3. _____

4. _____

5. _____

B. Using Active and Passive Voice

If humans ever colonize the moon or planets other than Earth, they must first figure out how the colony will be provided with water. Below, write a paragraph suggesting ways to bring, discover, or make water for use by a space colony. Your suggestions may be scientific or fantastic. Use at least two verbs in active voice and at least two verbs in passive voice. Make sure that the sentences with passive-voice verbs are not weak and would not sound better with active-voice verbs.

_____

_____

_____

_____

_____

_____

_____

_____

_____

_____

CHAPTER 6

Copyright © McDougal Littell Inc.

For use with Pupil's Edition pp. 141–142

Lesson 5

Shifts in Tense, Form, and Voice   *Reteaching*

Switch tenses, introduce progressive and emphatic forms, and change active into passive voice only as needed for clarity or style.

Combine different verb tenses and forms to show how events are related in time or to emphasize them differently.

Photography **had been** in existence for barely 30 years when the United States **was torn** by the Civil War. (A perfect tense and a simple tense are combined to provide a point of reference for the second event.)

Matthew Brady **photographed** people and scenes of the war while it **was being waged.** (A progressive tense and a simple tense are combined to show an ongoing action being interrupted by an event.)

Now, more than a century after the war **ended.** Brady's photographs **are** still a remarkable record of that tragic event. (Two simple tenses or some other combination of tenses is used to show different times of different actions.)

Stick with one tense when describing actions related to a single period or event or when writing about a series of events. When you change a verb from active to passive, the object of the verb becomes the subject of the sentence. The change alters the focus of the sentence.

Brady **uses** bulky equipment to develop the photos. (active voice, emphasis on *Brady*)

Bulky equipment **was used** to develop the photos. (passive voice, emphasis on the *equipment*)

Recognizing Errors in Verb Shift

Underline every verb in these sentences and watch for shifts in tense, form, and voice. Decide whether the shift within each item is correct. (The situation must fit one of the special cases described above.) Write **Correct** or **Incorrect.**

1. Although Brady's work produced the first battlefield photographs in this country, the earliest battlefield scenes had been shot a few years earlier. _____

2. Robert Fenton, a British journalist, took battlefield photographs during the Crimean War (1853–1856). Today he is recognized as a pioneer in photojournalism. _____

3. In those days, photographers had to process their photographic plates immediately after they take the photograph. _____

4. Therefore, when they were journeying through battlegrounds and over mountains, many photographers traveled in large wagons. _____

5. A photographer's wagon was used as a darkroom for developing his shots. With improvements to the process of photography, photographers had not needed to develop their own shots anymore. _____

CHAPTER 6

Lesson 5

Shifts in Tense, Form, and Voice

More Practice

Correcting Shifts in Tense, Form, and Voice

Rewrite each of the following sentences, changing the boldfaced verb to correct the unnecessary shift in tense, form, or voice. If the shift is needed for clarity, write **Correct**.

> **EXAMPLE** Lou will bring film and photos are being taken by Sara.
> *Lou will bring film and Sara will take photos.*

1. Photographs that were taken in the 1850s and 1860s **are giving** us a good idea of the world of that time.

   _____

   _____

2. Because modern systems of developing photos had not yet been invented, photographers of the day **take** large amounts of equipment with them.

   _____

   _____

3. In 1861, when two French photographers climbed to the top of Mont Blanc to shoot the scenery, 25 porters **were taken** along by them to carry their equipment.

   _____

   _____

4. What if you went on vacation and you **were having to take** 25 suitcases of camera equipment?

   _____

5. In America, photographs of the Western tribes **were taken** before their way of life changed.

   _____

6. Early photographers took portraits of people like President Abraham Lincoln and scientist John Hershel, who **has improved** photographic methods in his lifetime.

   _____

   _____

7. Each exposure took several minutes; a pose **was held** by the subject for that time.

   _____

8. The public **was shocked** into action by photographs that Jacob Riis was taking of New York City slums in 1888.

   _____

   _____

For use with Pupil's Edition pp. 143–145

CHAPTER 6

Lesson 5

Shifts in Tense, Form, and Voice

Application

A. Avoiding Shifts in Tense, Form, and Voice

As you read the first draft of an article you are writing, you notice that three of your sentences have unnecessary shifts in tense, form, and/or voice. Find the sentences with errors. Below, write the numbers of those sentences, and rewrite the sentences correctly.

(1) Margaret Bourke-White (1904–1971) was one of the most important photojournalists of the 20th century; she photographed industry in the United States and in the young Soviet Union, combat and concentration camps in World War II, and important events all over the world. (2) She was born in 1904, but her parents were raising her to think and act independently. (3) After graduating from college, where she studied photography, she moves to Cleveland and starts taking stunning photographs of steel mills and other industrial buildings. (4) In 1929, she joined the staff of a new business magazine; soon trips to Europe and Russia were being taken by her to photograph industry. (5) Her photos had already been awarded national attention when she began the most exciting part of her career with *Life*.

_____

_____

_____

_____

_____

_____

_____

_____

B. Using Shifts in Tense, Form, and Voice Correctly in Writing

Write about a time when you used your camera—or wished you had a camera—to record a memorable moment. Include each of the verb phrases listed below; underline them where they appear in your paragraph(s).

was taken   have talked   had known   was looking   will be keeping

_____

_____

_____

_____

_____

_____

CHAPTER 6

Lesson 6

The Mood of a Verb

Reteaching

The **mood** of a verb conveys the status of the action or condition it expresses. Verbs have three moods: indicative, subjunctive, and imperative.

Indicative. Use the indicative mood to make statements or ask questions.

> **Statement** The decorator hung paintings on the walls.

> **Question** How large is this room?

Subjunctive. Use the subjunctive mood to express a wish or state a condition that is contrary to fact. The subjunctive form is the same as the past form, except for the verb *be*. The subjunctive of *be* is *were*.

> I wish this house *were* mine.

You can use the subjunctive, in more formal communication, to express a command or request after the word *that*. In this case, the form of the verb is identical to its base form.

> The builder insisted that the sod *be* relaid.

Imperative. Use the imperative mood to make a request or give a command. This mood has only one tense, the present. Notice that the subject, *you,* is omitted.

> **Command** Be sure to go to the house tour.

A. Identifying the Mood of a Verb

Indicate the mood of each underlined verb. On the line, write **IND** for indicative, **IMP** for imperative, or **SUBJ** for subjunctive.

1. <u>Send</u> me a postcard from Vancouver. _____

2. <u>Did</u> you <u>finish</u> the report on time? _____

3. If I <u>were</u> you, I would write a letter to the editor. _____

4. <u>Let</u> me show you to your seat. _____

5. Only two people <u>were</u> in the store at the time. _____

6. The teacher asked that Marty <u>complete</u> the paper tonight. _____

7. He <u>had opened</u> the door too violently too many times. _____

8. Mel wishes he <u>were</u> invisible. _____

9. Please <u>tell</u> me what you think. _____

10. The plane <u>landed</u> just before midnight. _____

11. If I <u>were</u> governor, I would reduce taxes. _____

12. Kindly <u>take</u> the child's hand. _____

13. John asked that his name <u>be</u> removed from the mailing list. _____

(**For use with Pupil's Edition pp. 146–147**)

Lesson 6

The Mood of a Verb

More Practice

A. Identifying the Mood of a Verb

Indicate the mood of each underlined verb. On the line below each item, copy each underlined verb and label it with **IND** for indicative, **IMP** for imperative, or **SUBJ** for subjunctive.

> **EXAMPLE** <u>Tell</u> me how you would use the prize money if you <u>won</u>.
> *Tell, IMP; won, SUBJ*

1. Sometimes my neighborhood <u>is</u> so quiet that I <u>feel</u> as if I <u>were</u> the only person within miles.

   _____

2. <u>Think</u> what might happen if everyone <u>were</u> that careless!

   _____

3. Many times the penniless inventor <u>wished</u> he <u>had kept</u> the patent for his successful tool in his own name.

   _____

4. If people <u>were</u> able to fly like birds, where <u>would</u> we <u>place</u> the traffic lights?

   _____

5. The gangster <u>threatened</u>, "<u>Get</u> the money, or you'll wish you <u>were</u> dead."

   _____

6. The gangster <u>demanded</u> that the shopkeeper <u>pay</u> for "protection."

   _____

B. Using the Correct Mood of a Verb

Underline the correct form of the verb. On the line to the right, indicate which mood you used. Write **IND** for indicative, **IMP** for imperative, or **SUBJ** for subjunctive mood.

1. Please (return, returns) the books to the same places where you found them.   _____

2. Jeff wished he (was, were) the lead-off batter instead of a benchwarmer.   _____

3. Bettina reported she (was, were) at the drugstore.   _____

4. I wouldn't pay attention to him if he (grows, grew) another head!   _____

5. The rules of the game require that each player (waits, wait) for his or her turn before choosing a card.   _____

6. If Stanley (was, were) on the late bus, he probably stayed after class for a club meeting.   _____

CHAPTER 6

The Mood of a Verb

Application

A. Forming Different Moods of Verbs

Rewrite each sentence as indicated.

1. I request that you leave the room. (Change from indicative and subjunctive to imperative.)

_____

2. When Peg is mopping the floor, the radio is on. (Change from indicative to subjunctive.)

_____

3. If you were trying to impress me, you would move those bikes out of my way. (Change from subjunctive to imperative.)

_____

4. If a cat were in the room, he would start sneezing. (Change from subjunctive to indicative.)

_____

5. You would do well to remember these dates. (Change from indicative to imperative.)

_____

B. Using the Correct Mood in Writing

What superheroes have you read about or seen in cartoons or movies? If you could be a superhero, what special power would you choose to have? How would you use your power? Write a paragraph answering these questions. Include in your passage at least two verbs in the indicative mood, at least two in the imperative mood, and at least two in the subjunctive mood.

_____

_____

_____

_____

_____

_____

_____

_____

For use with Pupil's Edition pp. 146–147

Lesson 1 # Agreement in Number   *Reteaching*

A verb must agree with its subject in number. *Number* refers to whether a word is singular or plural. A singular subject takes a singular verb; a plural subject takes a plural verb.

> This **store sells** clothes for young people. (singular subject and verb)

> These **stores sell** a wide range of products. (plural subject and verb)

In a sentence with a verb phrase, the first helping verb agrees with the subject.

> Lately this **store has** been selling more videotapes than books.

A. Identifying Subjects and Verbs That Agree in Number

In each sentence, underline the subject and the verb. On the line following the sentence, write whether the two parts of the sentence **Agree** or **Disagree** in number.

1. My favorite bakery sell 12 different kinds of bagels.   _____

2. Brad spends hours at basketball practice.   _____

3. In weightlifting contests, competitors lifts heavy barbells.   _____

4. LaShauna enjoy her volunteer work with the Special Olympics.   _____

5. Often political parties hold rallies for their candidates.   _____

6. Tree trunks grow wider each year.   _____

7. Herpetologists studies reptiles and amphibians.   _____

8. During the holidays, the school choir perform at the local nursing home.   _____

9. The Weimaraner, a silver-grey hunting dog, is also known as "the Forester's dog."   _____

10. Veggie pizzas offers a wide choice of toppings.   _____

B. Making Subjects and Verbs Agree in Number

In each sentence, underline the verb that agrees with the subject.

1. Both countries (produces, produce) a surplus of meat and dairy products.

2. Sarah (commutes, commute) to her suburban school from the city center.

3. An elephant's skin (weighs, weigh) over a ton.

4. Your friends (holds, hold) afterschool jobs.

5. They (was, were) members of the winning team.

6. Virginia Woolf (is, are) the author of *To the Lighthouse*.

7. The Volta River (meets, meet) the sea on the south coast of Ghana.

8. Adult giraffes (grows, grow) to be about 18 feet tall.

9. The president (appoints, appoint) justices to the Supreme Court.

10. Grunions (is, are) small, silvery fish that live along the coast of California.

CHAPTER 7

Lesson 1

Agreement in Number

More Practice

A. Making Subjects and Verbs Agree in Number

In each blank, write the present tense form of the verb that agrees with the subject.

1. Violinists (draw) _____ a bow across the strings of their instruments.

2. Juan (tune) _____ the piano with a tuning fork.

3. Harps (contain) _____ as many as 47 strings.

4. Flutes (belong) _____ to the woodwind family of instruments.

5. Stephanie (play) _____ the clarinet in the school band.

6. Percussionists (strike) _____ their drums with a stick or mallet.

7. A synthesizer (create) _____ original sounds electronically.

8. Many rock musicians (use) _____ electric guitars and pianos.

9. A trombonist (pull) _____ the slide back and forth for the proper pitch.

10. The gong (signal) _____ the end of the performance.

B. Correcting Agreement Errors

Rewrite the paragraph below, making sure that all subjects and verbs agree.

(1) Stringed musical instruments are found around the globe.
(2) Americans think of the guitar, violin, and banjo as popular stringed instruments. (3) Chinese musicians plays the *ch' in* or the *pi-pa*. (4) In India, a musician strum the *sitar*. (5) Two stringed instruments enlivens Japanese music. (6) A player plucks the *koto* or the banjo-like *samisen*. (7) In the Middle East and North Africa, musicians use the *oud* and the *qanun*. (8) The African *sansa* is unique. (9) Its "strings" consists of metal strips. (10) Whatever its name, the stringed instrument enrich our musical world.

_____

_____

_____

_____

_____

_____

_____

_____

CHAPTER 7

For use with Pupil's Edition pp. 156–157

Lesson 1

Agreement in Number

Application

A. Proofreading for Errors in Agreement

Rewrite the paragraph below, making sure that all subjects and verbs agree.

The acronym laser stand for "light amplification by stimulated emission of radiation." Theodore H. Maiman's ruby laser were the first of these devices. A laser differ from fluorescent light or the sun. Lasers has a narrow light beam that is highly directional. Laser light vibrate at only one or very few frequencies. Other light sources has many frequencies. Laser beams cuts steel and fabric, reads supermarket labels, transmit television signals, and carry voice messages. In military operations laser beams bounces off a target and give information about the speed and distance of moving objects.

_____

_____

_____

_____

_____

_____

_____

_____

_____

B. Making Subjects and Verbs Agree in Writing

Choose one of the topics below and write a paragraph of at least five sentences about it. Make sure the subjects and verbs of all the sentences agree.

Some of my long-term goals
What I am looking for in a college
Benefits of volunteer work

Pros and cons of working an after-school job
My favorite extracurricular activities
A person who has had an impact on my life

_____

_____

_____

_____

_____

_____

_____

CHAPTER 7

Lesson 2

Phrases Between Subject and Verb

Reteaching

The subject of a verb is never part of a prepositional phrase, an appositive phrase, or a participial phrase. Such phrases may separate the subject from the verb. Remember that the number of the subject does not change. To find the subject, look at the words before the phrase. Make sure the verb agrees with the subject.

Prepositional Phrases

A **hive** <u>of lively bees</u> **is** noisy. (singular subject and verb)
The **bees** <u>in a hive</u> **communicate** with each other. (plural subject and verb)

Appositive Phrase

A bee's body **movements**, <u>a dance-like maneuver</u>, **give** other bees information about the location of pollen. (plural subject and verb)

Participial Phrase

The **bee**, <u>working slowly</u>, **completes** its task. (singular subject and verb)

A. Identifying Subjects and Verbs

Underline the subject and verb in each sentence. On the line, identify whether the subject and verb are **Singular** or **Plural**.

EXAMPLE The bee, as well as other insects, is useful to humans   *Singular*

1. Monarch butterflies, a member of the milkweed butterfly family, have an average wingspan of four inches.   _____

2. A dragonfly whose wings are outstretched is resting.   _____

3. A ladybug, also called a ladybird beetle, eats many harmful insects.   _____

4. Butterflies in their caterpillar stage are a source of food for birds and lizards.   _____

5. The number of wings differs between flies and bees.   _____

6. Boll weevils, a type of beetle, destroy many cotton crops yearly.   _____

7. Hordes of hungry grasshoppers strip any foliage in their path.   _____

8. An army of tiny ants marches toward the picnic basket.   _____

B. Making Subjects and Verbs Agree

Draw a line through any phrase that separates the subject from the verb. Underline the verb that agrees with the subject.

1. Twenty members of the marching band (has, have) arrived for practice.
2. The students, along with their art teacher, (is, are) going to the exhibition.
3. Jennifer, as well as many other tourists, (waits, wait) to kiss the Blarney Stone.
4. Peter Pan, one of James Barrie's characters, (runs, run) away to Neverland.
5. The sale of compact discs (has, have) risen at this store in the past year.
6. The decisions of the judge (comes, come) as no surprise.
7. Dark nimbus clouds in the summer sky often (foretells, foretell) a thunderstorm.

For use with Pupil's Edition pp. 158–159

CHAPTER 7

Lesson 2 # Phrases Between Subject and Verb   *More Practice*

A. Making Subjects and Verbs Agree

Underline the verb that agrees with the subject.

1. Insects in North America (includes, include) more than 100,000 species.
2. Stiletto-like mouthparts of the female mosquito (pierces, pierce) the victim's skin.
3. The millipede, or "insect with a thousand legs," actually (moves, move) on fewer than a hundred.
4. Wasps from the underground nest (is, are) swarming around the grill.
5. Worker fire ants (attacks, attack) poultry.
6. Caves around the world (holds, hold) many insects.
7. Borers, such as the carpenter ant, (causes, cause) great damage to wooden structures.
8. Insects of all types (outnumbers, outnumber) all other animals combined.
9. A Goliath beetle, one of the largest insects, (grows, grow) to four inches in length.
10. The lifespan of most insects (is, are) about a year.

B. Correcting Agreement in Number

In each of these sentences, decide whether the verb agrees with the subject in number. If it does, write **Correct** on the line. If it does not, cross out the incorrect verb and write the correct form of the verb on the line.

1. The distinctive wing pattern of Monarch butterflies identify them.   _____

2. Spiders, scorpions, mites, and ticks, is different types of Arachnids.   _____

3. Many types of vegetables depend on insect pollination.   _____

4. Ladybugs, one kind of beetle, devours many harmful insects.   _____

5. Maria, along with other campers, were bitten by mosquitoes.   _____

6. The mouthpart of certain insects define their method of eating.   _____

7. Often, moths in the woodlands blends into their surroundings.   _____

8. Tropical jungles, as well as the polar region, contains many species of insects.   _____

9. Honey from different hives tastes slightly different.   _____

10. At night, lights on the patio attracts insects.   _____

CHAPTER 7

Phrases Between Subject and Verb

Application

A. Correcting Agreement in Number

Locate the subject and verb of each numbered sentence. If there is an agreement error, write the subject and the correct form of the verb on the lines below. If the subject and verb agree, write **Correct.**

   (1) The term *insect community*, insects living together each with a defined job, usually signify ants and bees to most people. Termites form another such group. **(2)** Members with different jobs, such as royals, workers, and soldiers, works together for a smoothly-running society. **(3)** Workers, the greatest number in the community, do all the labor. Soldiers defend the group, and royals reproduce to keep it growing. **(4)** The nest of millions of termites consist of individual chambers, sometimes reaching mounds 20 feet high. **(5)** Raw materials, such as wood, is used to form the nest. Termites are found around the world. **(6)** Warmer regions in Africa and South America contains the largest communities.

1. _____

2. _____

3. _____

4. _____

5. _____

6. _____

B. Using Correct Subject-Verb Agreement

Write a paragraph using at least six sentences. Begin three of the sentences with any three of the following phrases. Throughout the paragraph, underline the subject and verb of each sentence. Make sure that each verb agrees in number with its subject.

A rainbow of gorgeous colors   Common pests in our country
Products such as honey   The size of insects
An essential part of ecosystems

_____

_____

_____

_____

_____

_____

For use with Pupil's Edition pp. 158–159

CHAPTER 7

Lesson 3

Compound Subjects

Reteaching

A **compound subject** is made up of two or more simple subjects joined by a conjunction. Compound subjects can take either singular or plural verbs.

My <u>brother and I</u> **are** both interested in cooking.

When the parts of a compound subject are joined by *or* or *nor,* the verb should agree with the part closest to it.

Either a large <u>tureen</u> or two smaller <u>bowls</u> **are needed** for the soup.
Neither the <u>grapes nor</u> the <u>banana</u> **is** ripe.

A. Making Verbs Agree with Compound Subjects

In each sentence, underline each part of the compound subject. Underline twice the word joining the parts. Then underline the verb in parentheses that agrees with the subject.

1. Culinary school and experience (are, is) necessary for becoming a chef.
2. Neither the ingredients nor the appearance (are, is) neglected in a fine dish.
3. Sometimes both professional chefs and amateurs (find, finds) cooking to be a challenge.
4. Either a microwave oven or conventional ovens (cause, causes) an unpierced potato to explode while baking.
5. Drizzled sauces or a handmade garnish (make, makes) Allen's creations unique.
6. Neither a pleasant atmosphere nor competent servers (bring, brings) customers to a restaurant if the food is bad.
7. Either the exotic fruits or the creamy custard (attract, attracts) me to this dessert.
8. (Do, Does) a white puffy hat and a white uniform still identify a person as a chef?
9. A bowl of soup or cups of coffee (have, has) boiled over in my microwave.
10. Neither frozen dinners nor a simple hot dog (survive, survives) intact if overcooked in a microwave.

B. Correcting Errors in Agreement

If the verb in a sentence does not agree with its compound subject, write the correct form of the verb on the line. If the verb does agree, write **Correct.**

1. Carnivals and amusement parks offers specialty foods. _____

2. Either frozen desserts or lemonade revive fair-goers on a hot summer day. _____

3. Fudge or lollipops delight many children and grown-ups. _____

4. Neither a hamburger nor fries seems right in this heat. _____

5. Soft pretzels and popcorn chase away the hunger pangs between meals. _____

CHAPTER 7

Compound Subjects

More Practice

A. Using the Correct Verb with a Compound Subject

On the line following each sentence, write the present tense form of the verb that agrees with the compound subject.

1. Cinnamon and other spices (add) spark to dishes. _____

2. Either crackers or a roll (come) with the soup. _____

3. Perhaps chocolate or strawberries (cause) Patty's allergic reactions. _____

4. Neither drink refills nor a senior citizen discount (be) available at this fast-food restaurant. _____

5. Peas and broccoli (head) George's list of least-favorite vegetables. _____

6. Peas or broccoli (find) its way into my family's menu at least once a week. _____

7. Neither the coach nor the players (know) what will be served at the sports banquet. _____

8. "Dog food and biscuits (taste) like cardboard," Oswald announced after he tried them. _____

9. Neither diet colas nor distilled water (contain) the sugar that other drinks do. _____

10. When Lee unexpectedly cooks for his wife, either fried eggs or an omelet (surprise) her. _____

11. Either rice or potatoes (coordinate) nicely with the main course. _____

12. Vitamin pills and fortified cereal (supply) much of a day's nutritional needs. _____

B. Correcting Errors in Agreement

Find the mistakes in the paragraph. Write the correct verb to agree with the subject. If the verb does agree, write **Correct.**

(1) Both my parents and I enjoy a good pizza. (2) Either four nearby pizza parlors or the closest supermarket provide us with our favorite carry-out food. (3) Plain cheese or vegetables are my mom's favorite toppings. (4) Either mushrooms or a combination of other veggies satisfy her. (5) Both sausage and pepperoni is at the top of Dad's list. (6) Because of my appreciation for every type of pizza, neither the vegetarian kind nor the meat pizzas are ever left.

1. _____   4. _____

2. _____   5. _____

3. _____   6. _____

For use with Pupil's Edition pp. 160–161

Lesson
3

Compound Subjects

Application

A. Combining Sentences Using Compound Subjects

Rewrite the following paragraph, using compound subjects.

There is an ice-cream flavor to please almost everyone. Fruit-flavored ice cream appeals to some people. Candy-flavored ice cream appeals to other people. Double Dark Chocolate captivates chocolate lovers. Chocolate Fudge Brownie ice cream captivates the so-called "chocaholic." Sorbets provide a nondairy alternative to ice cream. Sherbets, also, provide a lighter alternative to ice cream. Often a person with fragile teeth does not choose nutty ice cream. Similarly, a denture wearer does not choose flavors with nuts. A sauce adds to the delight of an ice-cream sundae. Sprinkles, like nuts or candy, are other popular additions. The old saying may be right: "We all scream for ice cream."

_____

_____

_____

_____

_____

_____

_____

_____

_____

_____

B. Using the Correct Verb with Compound Subjects

Write a public-service announcement concerning a food-related health or safety issue, such as the recall of some food product, a warning to boil water after a water-main break, an explanation of the food triangle, or the need to balance nutrients in a vegetarian diet. Use at least one example of each of these: a compound subject whose parts are joined by *and*; a compound subject whose parts are joined by *or* that takes a singular verb; and a compound subject whose parts are joined by *or* that takes a plural verb.

_____

_____

_____

_____

_____

CHAPTER 7

Name _____   Date _____

Lesson 4

Indefinite-Pronoun Subjects

Reteaching

When used as subjects, some indefinite pronouns are always singular. Examples include *another, anybody, anyone, each, everything, everyone, neither, nobody,* and *someone.* They take singular verbs.

> <u>Neither</u> of the mountain peaks <u>is</u> visible.

Some indefinite pronouns, including *both, few, several,* and *many,* are always plural. They take plural verbs.

> <u>Several</u> of the mountain climbers <u>carry</u> cameras.

Some indefinite pronouns, including *all, any, most, none,* and *some,* can be singular or plural depending on how they are used. If the pronoun refers to one person or thing, it takes a singular verb. If it refers to more than one person or thing, it takes a plural verb.

> <u>Most</u> of the <u>skiers</u> **are** from neighboring states. (There are many skiers.)
> <u>Most</u> of the <u>snow</u> **is** three feet deep. (The snow is considered as one unit.)

A. Identifying Indefinite Pronouns

In each sentence, underline the indefinite pronoun that appears as a subject. On the line, write whether the pronoun is **Singular** or **Plural.** If the pronoun can be either singular or plural, draw two lines under the word naming the person(s) or thing(s) it refers to.

> **EXAMPLE**   <u>None</u> of the <u>trees</u> are tall.   *Plural*
> <u>None</u> of the <u>scenery</u> is familiar.   *Singular*

1. Each of the Kenyan guides has been extremely helpful during the safari.   _____

2. Some of the tour buses visit Ottawa, Canada's capital.   _____

3. All of Greek culture's beauty is embodied in the elegant Parthenon.   _____

4. Several of the statistics about Mount Fuji are fascinating.   _____

5. In Moscow, most of the tourists recognize the domes of St. Basil's Cathedral.   _____

B. Making Indefinite Pronouns and Verbs Agree

In each sentence, underline the indefinite pronoun used as the subject. Then underline the verb form in parentheses that agrees with the subject.

> **EXAMPLE**   <u>Some</u> of the skiers (prefers, <u>prefer</u>) this trail.

1. Few of the world's ports (are, is) as busy as the harbors of Singapore.

2. All of the Amazon rainforest (are, is) home to unusual animals and birds.

3. Any of the visitors (recognize, recognizes) the 1,500-mile-long Great Wall of China.

4. Everyone (has, have) seen photos of the Great Sphinx.

5. Some of the glory of ancient Rome (are, is) still visible in the massive ruins.

6. Among the people on our tour, nobody (reports, report) anything lost or stolen.

CHAPTER 7

Copyright © McDougal Littell Inc.

(For use with Pupil's Edition pp. 162–163)

Lesson 4 — Indefinite-Pronoun Subjects

More Practice

A. Making Verbs Agree with Indefinite-Pronoun Subjects

Underline the subject of each sentence. Then underline the verb in parentheses that agrees with it in number.

1. Most of Saudi Arabia (consists, consist) of dry, barren land.
2. Unlike the planets, few of the planetary satellites (has, have) an atmosphere.
3. No one (sees, see) the Austrian Alps without being impressed by their beauty.
4. Some of the animal life we studied (lives, live) on land.
5. (Does, Do) any of the crew members have experience sailing in tropical storms?
6. Saved from developers, most of the marshland area (is, are) a wild preserve.
7. Many of the towns and villages in Alaska (has, have) airstrips for small planes.
8. None of the water in the neighboring towns (was, were) drinkable.
9. Each of the ducks (is, are) being tagged to trace its migration pattern.
10. Most of the jewelry diamonds (comes, come) from South Africa.
11. Neither of these jackets (fits, fit) me.
12. All of the dolls in period costumes (belongs, belong) on the second shelf.
13. None of the tomatoes (is, are) ripe yet.
14. At the sound of our footsteps, some of the squirrels (climbs, climb) the tree.
15. All of the evidence (supports, support) the defendant's alibi.

B. Using Verbs with Indefinite-Pronoun Subjects

Write the correct form of each numbered verb on the appropriate line below.

"In this slide, as you can see, everyone in the German Club **(1)** (board, boards) the airplane for the Frankfurt Airport." The German teacher clicked the control to bring up the next slide and explained it to the audience. "Several of the picturesque Bavarian villages **(2)** (is, are) found along this road out of Rothenburg, a charming medieval town. In Munich all of the tourists **(3)** (come, comes) to see the Glockenspiel, a tall tower with bells and moving puppets. Continuing into the Black Forest, our group climbs up a hill to Neuschwanstein. Most of that fairy-tale castle **(4)** (is, are) visible in this slide. Most of its tall spires **(5)** (shows, show) as white shapes against the green trees in this next shot. Some of the magic of famous Neuschwanstein **(6)** (have, has) been captured on souvenir puzzles, posters, and calendars," the teacher commented. "In the next slide, as the students view the remnants of the Berlin Wall, none of them **(7)** (speak, speaks) for a while, remembering the history of this area. That ends the slide show. If any of this report **(8)** (stirs, stir) you to travel, pick up our flyers concerning next year's trip."

1. _____   5. _____

2. _____   6. _____

3. _____   7. _____

4. _____   8. _____

CHAPTER 7

Lesson 4

Indefinite-Pronoun Subjects

Application

A. Checking Agreement of Verbs with Indefinite-Pronoun Subjects

Proofread this e-mail message for errors in subject-verb agreement. Underline any verb that does not agree with its subject.

I just got back from my trip to England. Almost all of the trip were exciting. The time on the plane was the only boring part. London, with all of its history and shopping and entertainment, were absolutely the best part of the trip! In London, we used public transportation. Many of the city buses are double-deckers, and most of the tourists climbs to the upper level for a good view. Rides on the Tube—London's subway—is faster, but nobody sees anything but walls down there. In England, getting across the streets are a little dangerous, because all of the traffic goes in the wrong direction—at least, everyone from America agree with that! None of my photos are developed yet. As soon as some is in my hands, I'll scan them in and send them to you.

B. Using Verbs Correctly with Indefinite Pronouns as Subjects

Think of a topic about which you can write a paragraph in which each of these phrases appears as the subject of a sentence. You may use the phrases in any order, and may write additional sentences with different subjects as well. Make sure each verb agrees with its subject. Write your paragraph on the lines below.

Both of them	Many of the scenes
None of the travelers	All of it
Everybody on the bus	Several of the others

_____

_____

_____

_____

_____

_____

_____

_____

_____

_____

_____

_____

For use with Pupil's Edition pp. 162–163

CHAPTER 7

Lesson 5 Other Problem Subjects   *Reteaching*

Sometimes the number of a subject can be hard to determine. To decide whether a subject takes a singular or plural verb, you sometimes need to decide whether the subject refers to a unit or to an individual. Here are some types of subjects that require special attention.

A **collective noun** refers to a group of people or things. Examples include *team, family, committee, jury, herd, class, staff*, and *majority*. When the members of the group act together, the collective noun takes a singular verb. When the members act as individuals, the collective noun takes a plural verb.

> The committee **meets** weekly. (acting as one)
> The committee **are** straggling into the office one at a time. (acting separately)

Some nouns ending in –s appear to be plural but are considered to be singular in meaning. Use singular verbs with these subjects. Examples include *news, measles, mumps, civics, mathematics, physics*, and *molasses*.

> Do you believe that bad news **travels** fast?

Some nouns ending in -ics such as *politics*, can be either singular or plural, depending on the context.

> Politics **is** a rough activity. The politics of getting re-elected **are** complicated.

Titles of works of art, literature, film, or music are considered singular. Similarly, words and phrases that refer to weights, measures, numbers, and lengths of time are usually treated as singular.

> *The Reivers,* by William Faulkner, **shows** the author's humorous side.
> Two thousand dollars **buys** a minute of commercial time on that program.
> Two hours on an airplane **is** all I can take.

Using Verbs That Agree with Problem Subjects

In each sentence, underline the subject and the form of the verb that agrees with it.

 1. The jury in this case (has, have) different opinions about a verdict.

 2. My family (is, are) planning to spend its vacation in Canada.

 3. The Student Activities Committee (reports, report) to the principal.

 4. Mathematics, the favorite subject of some students, (has, have) many divisions.

 5. Five pounds of potatoes (costs, cost) only a dollar during the sale.

 6. The cast (is, are) discussing their roles in the upcoming play.

 7. *Porgy and Bess* (is, are) the next production of the local theater group.

 8. Mumps (is, are) generally considered a disease of childhood.

 9. The crew of the airline (is, are) departing for Hawaii at noon.

10. "Quiet Nights" (was, were) a popular instrumental record during her school days.

11. Pediatrics (has, have) been selected as his area of specialization.

12. Two teaspoons of salt (seems, seem) like an unhealthy amount for this dish.

13. His business ethics (seems, seem) sharply different from mine.

14. The election news (was, were) on the front page of the paper.

15. Your pliers (is, are) on the workbench.

CHAPTER 7

Lesson 5 # Other Problem Subjects   *More Practice*

A. Using Verbs That Agree with Problem Subjects

In each sentence, underline the verb that agrees in number with the subject.

1. The flock of geese (is, are) flying in the normal v-formation.
2. After all these years in print, *The Adventures of Sherlock Holmes* (holds, hold) the reader's attention.
3. The ethics of the two dozen fake doctors (is, are) are certainly questionable.
4. The crew (takes, take) shore leave at various times so the ship is never left shorthanded.
5. Four hours (is, are) too long to stand in line, even for a roller coaster.
6. Mathematics (is, are) her current major, but she's also considering chemistry.
7. The staff (has, have) not yet returned their questionnaires.
8. The family (rents, rent) a cottage on the lake every year.
9. The news about Grandma's surgery (encourages, encourage) us so far.
10. Three pounds of lunchmeat (is, are) more than enough for the picnic.

B. Writing Sentences

Complete each of these sentences by adding a verb as described in the parentheses and any other needed words.

EXAMPLE (plural verb) The flock of geese *are separating into three groups.*

1. (singular verb) A volunteer army _____
_____

2. (plural verb) A volunteer army _____
_____

3. (plural verb) My soccer team _____
_____

4. (singular verb) My soccer team _____
_____

5. (singular verb) The men's chorus _____
_____

6. (plural verb) The men's chorus _____
_____

For use with Pupil's Edition pp. 164–166

CHAPTER 7

Other Problem Subjects _Application_

A. Proofreading for Subject-Verb Agreement

Proofread this paragraph for errors in subject-verb agreement. Underline any verb that does not agree with its subject.

The Festival of Film Classics are scheduled for six weeks from now, and this planning committee still have a great deal of work to do. Everyone sees that a few of our group is missing. Measles are keeping Dot home in bed, and the news about Robbie's broken arm have been heard by all of us. However, the majority of our members is here, so let's begin. One hundred fifty dollars have been budgeted for the advertising campaign. Fortunately, the staff of the school paper has offered to do what they can to get the word out. The other good news is about the student film competition. Now that Dr. Pratt has agreed to serve, the jury are complete. Next, we need to finalize the schedule of movies. _The Best Years of Our Lives_ is set for our opening film, representing the 1940s. _Wings_ have been selected from the 1920s. The team selecting the movie for the 1930s are still debating the possibilities. Have the other teams made their choices? Six weeks are not much time for completing the arrangements!

B. Writing Original News Articles for Headlines

In the headlines below, note the difference in verb form in each pair. Choose one pair to write about and cross out the other pair. Then write two articles, one for each headline in the chosen pair, that illustrate the difference in meaning signified by the different verbs.

Jury Makes Statements
Staff Wins Awards

Jury Make Statements
Staff Win Awards

_____   _____

_____   _____

_____   _____

_____   _____

_____   _____

_____   _____

_____   _____

_____   _____

_____   _____

_____   _____

_____   _____

CHAPTER 7

Lesson
6

Special Sentence Problems

Reteaching

Making a verb agree with its subject can be tricky when the subject is difficult to identify. The subject is often hard to find in sentences where it follows the verb or comes between parts of the verb. In many questions, subjects follow verbs or come between parts of verb phrases. To find the subject in a question, rewrite the sentence as a statement.

In sentences beginning with *here* or *there,* the subjects usually follow the verb. *Here* or *there* rarely function as subjects.

In an **inverted sentence,** the subject follows the verb. Notice, with the examples below, how reordering the words in standard order helps you find the subject.

Question:	**Does** <u>Independence Day</u> **fall** on Friday this year?
	<u>Independence Day</u> **does fall** on Friday this year.
***Here* or *There*:**	There **are** the <u>fireworks</u>.
	The <u>fireworks</u> **are** there.
Inverted order:	Into the sky **shoots** a whining <u>rocket</u>.
	A whining <u>rocket</u> **shoots** into the sky.

A **predicate nominative** is a noun or pronoun that follows a linking verb and describes the subject. The verb must agree with the subject, not the predicate nominative. In these examples, the subject is underlined once; the predicate nominative is underlined twice.

My favorite <u>activity</u> on the Fourth of July **is** the <u><u>picnics</u></u>.

The <u>picnics</u> **are** my favorite <u><u>activity</u></u>.

The verb in an **adjective clause** must agree in number with the relative pronoun (examples: *that, which,* or *who*) that is the subject of the clause. In these sentences, the pronoun that is the subject of the adjective clause is underlined once. Its antecedent is underlined twice.

The <u><u>contestants</u></u> <u>who</u> **run** in the race have a lot of energy.

The <u><u>contestant</u></u> <u>who</u> **runs** the fastest gets a prize.

Solving Agreement Problems

In each sentence, find and underline the subject of the boldfaced verb.

1. Across our country **are celebrated** countless religious, ethnic, and national holidays.

2. These specially-built stands **are** the best place to see the July 4 fireworks.

3. Down the street **march** the veterans taking part in the Memorial Day parade.

4. Christmas trees, originally lit with candles, **were** a German innovation.

5. When a one-day supply of oil kept temple lamps burning for eight days, then **was born** Chanukah, the Festival of Lights.

6. My friend Maleek, who **is** Muslim, celebrates at the end of the month of Ramadan.

7. For how many years **has** Kwanzaa **been celebrated?**

8. Every May 5, there **is** a festive remembrance of a Mexican victory and Mexican independence in the "Cinco de Mayo" celebration.

(**For use with Pupil's Edition pp. 167–169**)

Special Sentence Problems

More Practice

A. Solving Agreement Problems

In each sentence, find and underline the subject. Then underline the form of the verb that agrees with the subject.

1. There (comes, come) a time when we should consider our abilities and set goals.

2. Near the Thames in London (is, are) the monument commemorating the Great Fire.

3. What (is, are) the price of those CB radio kits?

4. In the swamp at the edge of the lagoon (grows, grow) mangrove trees.

5. A Korean tradition (is, are) special birthday celebrations at 100 days old, one year old, and 60 years old.

6. Down on our farm (lives, live) sheep, goats, cows, horses, and chickens.

7. Where (is, are) the book of photographs by Ansel Adams?

8. The letters on the table (is, are) what arrived today.

9. My brother is the leader of those boys who (does, do) odd jobs.

10. Here in this package (is, are) your secret documents.

B. Correcting Agreement Errors

Decide whether the verb in each sentence agrees with the subject. If it does, write **Correct** on the line to the right. If it does not, write the correct form on the line.

1. Where is the copy of the original Magna Carta? _____

2. The range of this unique singer's voice was five octaves. _____

3. Across the bay, from San Francisco to Sausalito, extend the Golden Gate Bridge. _____

4. There is a small boy and his father at the door. _____

5. Down from the Rocky Mountains blow a warm, dry wind called a chinook. _____

6. Why does Switzerland have three official languages? _____

7. Near the state border lies the three small lakes formed by glaciers. _____

8. The problem with those bright lamps are fire hazards. _____

9. Through which European cities do the Volga River flow? _____

10. What are the sweaters that Irish fishermen wear called? _____

CHAPTER 7

Special Sentence Problems

Application

Revising for Sentence Variety and Agreement

Almost every sentence in the following paragraph is written in an unusual subject-verb pattern. The effect is stilted writing. In addition, several sentences have errors in subject-verb agreement. Revise the paragraph to sound more natural by using normal subject-verb order in a few of the sentences. Remember to make all verbs agree with their subjects.

> Costume parties held to celebrate Halloween, Mardi Gras, or no holiday at all is great entertainment. At a costume party imagine yourself. Masquerading as tubes of toothpaste are a pair of young women. On their heads sit lampshade "caps." Does cardboard boxes ever turn into a costume? One young man with big ideas, who wear a painted refrigerator box, is an office building. Here come someone wearing three hula hoops at different angles. The exact opposite of the walking office building is he. Whirling about him are electron trails, for he's a tiny atom. There, next to the refreshments, are a young woman wearing her clothes backwards. Over her face is combed locks of her hair, and on the back of her head rides a mask. Having fun is all of the guests except the backwards woman. Confused are everyone else about whether to talk to her front or her back.

_____

_____

_____

_____

_____

_____

_____

_____

_____

_____

_____

_____

_____

_____

_____

For use with Pupil's Edition pp. 167–169

Nominative and Objective Cases

Reteaching

Lessons 1–2

Personal pronouns change case depending on how they function in a sentence. Use the **nominative form** of a personal pronoun when the pronoun functions as a subject or a predicate nominative. A nominative pronoun may be used as part of a compound subject.

Nominative	First Person	Second Person	Third Person
Singular	I	you	he, she, it
Plural	we	you	they
Objective			
Singular	me	you	him, her, it
Plural	us	you	them

Subject	<u>I</u> read about Gonzalo Pizarro and Francisco de Orellana.
Part of compound subject	Pizarro and <u>he</u> were searching for gold.

When you must choose the correct pronoun case in a compound subject, first try each part of the compound subject alone in the sentence, and then choose the correct case for the sentence.

Alfredo and (I, me) drew a cartoon.   <u>I</u> drew a cartoon. (correct)
<u>Me</u> drew a cartoon. (incorrect)   <u>Alfred and I</u> drew a cartoon.

A nominative pronoun used as a predicate nominative is called a **predicate pronoun.** It immediately follows a linking verb and identifies the subject of the sentence.

Predicate pronoun It was <u>he</u> who became the first Spaniard to travel the length of the Amazon River.

Use the **objective form** of a personal pronoun when the pronoun functions as a direct object, indirect object, or object of a preposition. Also use it when the pronoun is part of a compound object.

Direct object	Orellana joined <u>them</u> east of Quito, Equador.
Indirect object	Pizarro gave <u>him</u> specific instructions.
Object of preposition	Surviving the journey became difficult for <u>them</u>.
Part of compound object	The river posed dangers for Orellana and <u>them</u>.

Similar to compound subjects, when you must choose the correct pronoun case in a compound object, look at each part of the object separately.

Identifying the Case of a Pronoun

Underline the correct pronoun to complete each sentence.

1. Orellana and (they, them) endured many hardships on their trip.

2. At one point, they saw women warriors who attacked (them, they) ruthlessly.

3. Friar Carvajal was traveling with Orellana, and it was (him, he) who called the women Amazons because they reminded him of a Greek story of fighting women.

4. Orellana traveled the entire length of the huge river. Instead of being named for (he, him), the river was named after the unusual warriors who had attacked him.

CHAPTER 8

Nominative and Objective Cases

More Practice

A. Using the Correct Case of Personal Pronouns

Underline the correct form from the pronouns in parentheses.

1. After Europeans heard about the riches in America, they spent years and fortunes trying to find (they, them).

2. For example, Europeans heard a myth about a place called El Dorado: There the king covered himself with gold dust each day, and (him, he) and his people threw gold into a lake.

3. When Spanish conquistadors Orellana and Pizarro began their trip in 1541, (they, them) were searching for El Dorado.

4. Sir Walter Raleigh, a friend of Queen Elizabeth of England, became fascinated by the tale, and he searched for El Dorado to bring gold back to England and (she, her).

5. Although there is no El Dorado, a tribe called Muisca may have thrown gold offerings into a lake in Colombia; to (them, they) the lake was sacred.

6. Historians tell (we, us) that no one ever found the legendary El Dorado.

7. European explorers were also fascinated by the story of the Fountain of Youth, told to (them, they) by native people.

8. If a man drank from the fountain, they said, (he, him) would have eternal youth.

9. Juan Ponce de León determined to find the fountain; it was (he, him) who is associated most closely with the search.

10. (He, Him) and his followers searched for the Fountain in Florida, but it never appeared to (him, he) and (they, them).

B. Choosing Personal Pronouns

Fill in the blanks in the following sentences with appropriate personal pronouns. Vary the person and number of the pronouns, and do not use the pronoun *you*.

1. The Chungs and _____ missed the first scene of the play.

2. The co-chairpersons of the committee are Harold and _____.

3. Just between you and _____, I'm afraid of flying in an airplane.

4. Anita told Leon and _____ that she will finish the project on time.

5. Our friends and _____ will travel to Spain this summer.

6. We lost the ball to _____ in the final quarter.

7. _____ and _____ belong to the debate club.

8. Show the program to Mrs. Brown and _____ before you have it copied.

9. Uncle Tom helped _____ repair my car.

10. Was it _____ you saw at the football game last Friday?

For use with Pupil's Edition pp. 178–182

Nominative and Objective Cases

Lessons 1–2

Application

A. Proofreading

Proofread the following story to make sure that the correct cases of pronouns have been used. When you find a pronoun used incorrectly, cross it out. Then insert this proofreading symbol ∧ and write the correct pronoun above it.

Spanish conquistadors were obsessed with the search for gold. That obsession took him to remote parts of the Americas. According to one story they had heard, there were seven golden cities somewhere in the area that is now Arizona and New Mexico. In the mythical Seven Golden Cities of Cíbola, the walls were made of gold and decorated with turquoise. The story can be traced back to an imaginative man named Friar Marcos de Niza. It was him who first told the story to his provincial governor. The governor assigned Francisco Vazquez de Coronado to find the cities. Him and a group of soldiers, slaves, and priests set out with Friar Marcos to find the Seven Golden Cities of Cíbola in 1540.

Coronado and his expedition traveled with Friar Marcos for months throughout the dry, dusty lands of the Southwest and found no golden cities. Friar Marcos eventually found himself in danger. After months of aimless wandering, an intense resentment had developed between Coronado's men and he. The men felt that he had misled them, and Coronado was forced to send the friar back home, for fear of reprisal against he. Coronado and his men searched in vain, but all it could find was a few poor Zuni villages. With respect to finding gold, the expedition was a failure. However, the men must have been impressed by one experience they had during this time, when their leader and them sighted the Grand Canyon. They were the first Europeans to see this natural wonder.

B. Using Pronouns in Writing

Write an original legend or myth about a person who discovers a place of great wealth. Be sure to use personal pronouns correctly. Use a separate piece of paper if necessary.

_____

_____

_____

_____

_____

CHAPTER 8

The Possessive Case

Reteaching

Personal pronouns that show ownership or relationship are in the **possessive case.**

	First Person	Second Person	Third Person
Singular	my, mine	your, yours	his, her, hers, its
Plural	our, ours	your, yours	their, theirs

A possessive pronoun can be used in place of a noun. Some of these pronouns can function as subjects or objects.

> Families often move to new houses. <u>Mine</u> moved last weekend. Didn't the movers move <u>yours</u> recently?

A possessive pronoun can be used to modify a noun or a gerund. The pronoun comes before the noun or gerund it modifies.

> <u>Our</u> moving has caused me to lose many important items.

Some contractions and possessive pronouns sound alike, but they have different spellings and meanings.

<u>You're</u> strong!   Here is <u>your</u> bed.
<u>They're</u> packing boxes.   The movers are using <u>their</u> dolly.
<u>There's</u> my bed.   That bed is <u>theirs</u>.
<u>It's</u> exciting.   The moving company brought <u>its</u> biggest van.

Identifying Possessive Pronouns

Underline the possessive pronouns in the following sentences.

1. When people move, their world is turned upside down for a while.
2. Even if you plan the move carefully, many of your possessions end up lost.
3. For example, when my family moved, we lost our best dishes.
4. My sister lost her shoes, but luckily I kept track of mine.
5. Unfortunately, my father still can't find his toolbox.
6. When my friend's family moved, they lost something unusual—their dog.
7. I guess their dog missed its old friends, so it ran away from the new home.
8. On top of the difficulties associated with moving, the family had to run an ad about their lost dog.
9. One person phoned them, saying she had found a dog; she asked my friend to describe his dog.
10. After hearing his description, she said, "I think this dog must be yours. Can you come and get him?"
11. It turned out that the dog she found wasn't his after all.
12. However, an old neighbor found the dog wandering around its old house and kindly returned it to its family.
13. The dog was still unhappy, and you could hear its barking and howling at night for about a week.
14. Compared with that situation, the story of our moving was easy.
15. After all, ours was at least quiet, even if we temporarily lost a few items.

For use with Pupil's Edition pp. 183–184

Lesson 3

The Possessive Case

More Practice

A. Identifying Possessive Pronouns

Underline the correct form of the pronoun from those given in parentheses.

1. Recent statistics say that Americans change (they're, their) residences about every seven years.

2. (My, Mine) grandparents have lived in their home for over 50 years.

3. I wonder if the experts included my grandparents in (their, they're) figures.

4. A friend of (my, mine) said that (his, he) family moved here from California.

5. His home is newer than (our, ours); in fact, it was just built.

6. Our home was built in 1924; (theirs, their) was built last year.

7. When was (your, yours) home built?

8. One of (my, mine) friends has moved to a condo in Chicago.

9. (Her, Hers) mother is glad that she doesn't have to do yard work anymore.

10. (They're, Their) old house had a big yard to care for and a long driveway to shovel in the winter.

11. I keep forgetting (their, theirs) new address.

12. Her parents are enjoying their new home, but (my, mine) like our home just fine.

13. Even with (its, it's) problems, it's still the home we love.

14. If (you're, your) goal is to make a new beginning, maybe moving is a good idea.

B. Using Pronouns Correctly

Fill in the blanks in the following sentences with appropriate possessive pronouns.

1. I can't read the words on that sign because _____ print is too small.

2. When I saw my neighbor wash his car, I decided to wash _____ too.

3. If _____ ticket wins the lottery, you will be rich.

4. That university is famous for _____ tradition of fine academics.

5. Both ballplayers have dirtied _____ uniforms by sliding into second base.

6. Jason is glad that _____ diving has improved so much this year.

7. Bernice, I found this ring beside the sink; is it _____ or _____?

8. This cartoon always reflects _____ creator's political views.

9. We have decided that the cat we found will be _____ if no one claims it soon.

10. Mrs. Jackson has been trying not to lose _____ temper as much lately.

CHAPTER 8

The Possessive Case

Application

A. Proofreading for Pronoun Errors

Proofread the following carelessly written paragraph, looking for errors in possessive pronoun usage. When you find a possessive pronoun used incorrectly, cross it out. Then insert this proofreading symbol ∧ and write the correct pronoun above it.

In you history classes, did you ever learn about Montezuma II and his great empire in Mexico? Did you learn about the tragic end to his reign? Montezuma II was the great-grandson of Montezuma I, who had been the emperor of the Aztecs around 1450. Like their grandfather, Montezuma II ruled the Aztec empire from the capital city Tenochtitlán, now Mexico City. Ours history books tell us that during Montezuma II's reign, many public works, such as water conduits, hospitals, and temples were built. Montezuma did his best to rule the vast empire wisely. However, when the Spaniards under Hernando Cortés landed in Mexico, her reign abruptly ended.

At first, Montezuma welcomed Cortés, giving him golden gifts. Montezuma and some of their subjects thought that Cortés was the god Quetzalcóatl who had returned to his people. Soon, however, Cortés, taking advantage of the trust Montezuma had placed in him, captured the Aztecs' capital city and they're emperor. Through there deceit, the Spaniards were able to conquer the entire empire. Perhaps their code of conduct allowed them to treat people in this way. By mine standards, though, they acted dishonorably.

B. Using Pronoun Cases Correctly in Writing

Write a paragraph about a time when you or your family moved. If you've never moved, write a paragraph describing an imaginary move. Use the correct cases of personal pronouns in your sentences. Be sure to use at least five pronouns in the possessive case. Use a separate piece of paper if necessary.

_____

_____

_____

_____

_____

_____

_____

For use with Pupil's Edition pp. 183–184

Using *Who* and *Whom*

Reteaching

The case of the pronoun *who* is determined by the pronoun's function in the sentence.

Nominative	Objective	Possessive
who, whoever	whom, whomever	whose, whosever

Who and *whom* can be used to ask questions and to introduce subordinate clauses.

Who is the nominative form. In a question, *who* is used as a subject or as a predicate pronoun. *Whom* is the objective form. In a question, *whom* is used as a direct or indirect object of a verb or as the object of a preposition.

Subject	<u>Who</u> discovered the tomb of King Tut?
Predicate nominative	The explorer was <u>who</u>?
Object	With <u>whom</u> did Howard Carter work?

This is how to use *who* and *whom* when introducing subordinate clauses. When the pronoun functions as the subject in a subordinate clause, use *who*. When the pronoun functions as the object in a subordinate clause, use *whom*.

Subject of clause	It was Howard Carter <u>who</u> found the door of the tomb.
Object in clause	The ruler <u>whom</u> the ancient Egyptians buried in the tomb was Tutankhamen.

Using *Who* and *Whom* Correctly

Choose the correct pronoun from those in parentheses in the following sentences.

1. (Who, Whom) was Tutankhamen?

2. Before and after (who, whom) did he reign?

3. King Tut was a young king (who, whom) ascended the throne when he was only nine years old.

4. Aton was the single god (whom, who) the people of Egypt worshiped at that time.

5. Although King Tut believed in Aton, there were many priests in Egypt (whose, whom) beliefs ran counter to the King's.

6. After Tut's death and burial, priests (who, whom) rejected Aton tried to destroy all monuments to the young king.

7. By (who, whom) was King Tut remembered after centuries?

8. Archaeologist Howard Carter, for (who, whom) researching ancient Egypt was a lifelong obsession, found the tomb of King Tut while digging at the entrance to a nearby tomb.

9. The people who stocked the tomb left both useful and beautiful things to be used in the afterlife by the king (who, whom) they respected and admired.

10. Carter, (who, whose) reaction was great joy, was amazed at what he found.

11. (Whoever, Whomever) had filled the tomb had left a variety of precious and historical objects, such as model ships, carved statues, gold jewelry, and weapons.

12. (Who, Whom) believes in the so-called curse of King Tut?

Lesson 4

Using *Who* and *Whom*

More Practice

A. Identifying the Function of *Who* and *Whom*

In the following sentences, identify the function of *who* or *whom*. If a sentence uses *who*, underline once the verb of which it is the subject. If a sentence uses *whom*, underline twice the verb or preposition of which it is an object.

EXAMPLES I read about people **who** had been born on my birthday.
One of them is someone about **whom** we have all heard.

1. **Whom** do you know in Denver, Colorado?
2. The new principal will be **whomever** the school board supports.
3. Do you know **who** won the election?
4. The salesclerk to **whom** you spoke yesterday is working with another customer.
5. The artist **who** painted this portrait captured an unusual expression.
6. Was John Adams the president **who** was the first to live in the White House?
7. **Whom** will you choose as your lab partner in chemistry?
8. The operator **whom** I called gave me important information.

B. Using *Who* and *Whom* Correctly

Choose the correct pronoun from those in parentheses in the following sentences.

1. The workers (who, whom) had been digging in the desert heat were tired.
2. (Whom, Who) expected them to find this treasure, almost untouched for centuries?
3. (Whoever, Whosever) dream it was to find the tomb of King Tut had inspired their employers.
4. The king (who, whose) death happened centuries ago is now known worldwide.
5. Howard Carter, the archaeologist (who, whom) made the discovery, was excited.
6. He contacted the man from (who, whom) he had received financial backing, Lord George Edward Carnarvon, in England.
7. By (who, whom) had the royal seal been affixed to the wall so many years ago?
8. The first person to look inside was (who, whom)?
9. Carter himself, (who, whom) had searched for years, was given the privilege.
10. He was the one (who, whom) reported that he caught the glint of gold.
11. (Whoever, Whomever) had filled the tomb wanted to insure King Tut's happiness in the afterlife.
12. Carter was a scientist (who, whose) dedication we should all admire.
13. Six weeks after entering the tomb, one of the searchers (who, whom) had entered the tomb died of a blood infection.
14. Others (who, whom) had been involved in the discovery supposedly committed suicide.
15. Howard Carter dismissed all rumors of a curse; he was one of those logical people to (who, whom) superstitions made no sense.

For use with Pupil's Edition pp. 185–187

CHAPTER 8

Using *Who* and *Whom*
Application

A. Proofreading for *Who* and *Whom*

Proofread the following paragraph. When you find the pronoun *who, whom,* or *whose* used incorrectly, cross it out. Then insert this proofreading symbol ʌ and write the correct pronoun above it.

Who knows why the magnificent Mayan civilization of Central America collapsed over a thousand years ago? The Maya, who we credit with achievements in the fields of architecture, astronomy, mathematics, and the arts, peaked as a civilization around A.D. 250. The Maya were the people whom understood the movement of the sun and stars better than anyone else at the time. They made a calendar whose basis was the 365-day orbit of the earth around the sun. The Maya are also the people whom many historians believe first invented the zero. Whomever sees the inscribed stone monuments in the ruins of their ancient cities is looking at an original system of writing. Students, especially those for who history is the highest interest, will continue to wonder why the Mayan civilization declined.

B. Using *Who, Whom,* and *Whose* in Writing

Rewrite each sentence or pair of sentences below as a single sentence that uses a subordinate clause introduced by or containing *who, whom,* or *whose.* Use the pronoun given in parentheses in your new sentence.

EXAMPLE I just met the homeowner; she tends this beautiful garden. (who)
I just met the homeowner who tends this beautiful garden.

1. Charles Dickens was a popular author in 19th century England; he released many of his stories in serial format to keep his audience interested for months. (who)

_____

_____

2. Franklin Roosevelt was a powerful president, and his ideas were fresh and innovative. (whose)

_____

3. Pierre and Marie Curie were scientists; they discovered radium. (who)

_____

4. Do you remember the name of that tutor? You called her on Thursday night. (whom)

_____

CHAPTER 8

Pronoun-Antecedent Agreement *Reteaching*

A pronoun must agree with its antecedent in number, gender, and person. An **antecedent** is the noun or pronoun that a pronoun refers to or replaces.

If the antecedent is singular, use a singular pronoun. If it is plural, use a plural pronoun.

> Mrs. Brady works in the school office. Students often approach her desk.

> Some students are confused, and they hope she can help.

Here are three trouble spots that often confuse writers and readers.

- A collective noun such as *band* may be referred to by either a singular or a plural pronoun, depending upon its meaning in the sentence.

  > The band boarded its bus in front of the school. (singular)
  > The band wore their full dress uniforms on cool nights. (plural)

- A plural pronoun is used to refer to nouns or pronouns joined by *and*.

  > The principal and the superintendent voiced their opinions at the meeting.

- A pronoun that refers to nouns or pronouns joined by *or* or *nor* should agree with the noun or pronoun nearest to it.

  > Neither the coach nor the players have made up their minds.

The **gender** of the pronoun—masculine (*he, his, him*), feminine (*she, her, hers*), or neuter (*it, its*)—must be the same as the gender of its antecedent. The **person** (first, second, third) of the pronoun must agree with the person of its antecedent.

> She wears a blue sweater that matches her eyes.

> You look good in the blue sweater that matches your eyes.

Identifying Pronouns and Their Antecedents

In each sentence underline the pronoun once and the antecedent twice.

1. The school office is open all day, and it is often a busy place.
2. The principal says his door is always open.
3. Indeed, as most students know, the principal has proven many times that he can be counted on in any emergency.
4. Mrs. Brady, the school secretary, usually answers her phone hundreds of times every day.
5. Each teacher has his or her own mailbox for important messages.
6. All teachers check their mailboxes at least once a day.
7. When parents have concerns, they stop by the office.
8. Students who have had difficulties in classrooms often find themselves waiting on a bench in the office for a while before talking to the assistant principal.
9. When the local fire chief wants to check the school's fire preparedness, she checks in at the office first.
10. When Kristen felt ill last month, she waited in the office until her mother came to pick her up.
11. Once, when a dog was found in the building, students brought it to the office while the owner was notified.

For use with Pupil's Edition pp. 188–190

CHAPTER 8

Pronoun-Antecedent Agreement
More Practice

A. Identifying Pronouns and Their Antecedents
In each sentence draw an arrow to connect each pronoun with its antecedent.

1. The custodian takes his responsibility as caretaker of the building seriously.
2. Ms. Johnson completed training before earning her job as fireperson.
3. When students pass Mr. Price, the hall monitor, he checks to see where they are going and whether they have a hall pass.
4. In the cafeteria, the workers cook the food, and they fill the students' plates.
5. Security officers quickly learn about the school and its schedules.
6. Mr. Gray, a school counselor, posts his office hours on his door.
7. When a student feels ill, the school nurse can help; she provides students a quiet place to rest.
8. All employees feel it is their responsibility to keep the school running efficiently.
9. The art teacher displays outstanding work from his class in the hall.
10. The coach and the basketball team are proud to see their names on the plaque.

B. Making Pronouns and Antecedents Agree
Underline the pronoun that correctly completes each sentence. Then underline the antecedent(s) of the pronoun.

1. The audience found (his or her, their) seats again after intermission.
2. Yesterday the Institute of Art held a reception to celebrate (their, its) third anniversary.
3. Has every attendee brought (his or her, your) own lunch?
4. Is the football team satisfied with (their, its) new locker room?
5. Each passenger is responsible for (their, his or her) own luggage.
6. Neither Megan nor her sisters remembered (her, their) lunches.
7. The team stood at attention during the national anthem with (its, their) hands over (its, their) hearts.
8. The band quickly assembled at the 50-yard line, where (they, it) lifted their instruments and began to play.
9. Neither the runners-up nor the winner has had (her, their) name announced.
10. Ariel and Blake explained (his or her, their) project to the class.
11. Has either Emily or Gwen received (their, her) award yet?
12. Without a good night's sleep, a student can't be at (your, his or her) best.
13. Was it Plato or Aristotle who had Alexander the Great as one of (their, his) pupils?
14. The family from Russia celebrates holidays (their, its) own way.
15. All drivers should have (his or her, their) eyes checked regularly.

Pronoun-Antecedent Agreement

Application

A. Making Pronouns and Antecedents Agree in Writing

Read the following paragraph. Look especially for errors in agreement between pronouns and their antecedents. Rewrite the numbered sentences correctly on the corresponding lines below.

     (1) Caricature, the art of making satirical portraits, has their roots in 17th-century Italy. During the 18th century, the comic art of caricature flourished in England in literature as well as in art. **(2)** Neither the artists nor the writers based his caricatures solely on grim reality. Charles Dickens is a famous literary caricaturist. **(3)** Many of Dickens's characters remain in our memories because of his exaggerated appearances and mannerisms. Modern political cartoons are another type of caricature. **(4)** Few cartoonists want his work to hurt the politician; cartoonists intend only to expose follies and foibles. **(5)** In order to draw a successful caricature, an artist must train their eye to select the feature that should be exaggerated or distorted.

1. _____

2. _____

3. _____

   _____

4. _____

   _____

5. _____

   _____

B. Writing with Pronouns

Write a description of a few of the many people who work in your school. Describe what they do to keep the school running efficiently. Be sure to include at least five personal pronouns with clear antecedents.

_____

_____

_____

_____

_____

_____

For use with Pupil's Edition pp. 188–190

Copyright © McDougal Littell Inc.

Lesson 6

Indefinite Pronouns as Antecedents

Reteaching

When an indefinite pronoun is the antecedent of a personal pronoun, the personal pronoun must agree in number with the indefinite pronoun. The number of an indefinite pronoun is not always obvious.

Indefinite Pronouns

Singular			Plural	Singular or Plural
another	everybody	no one	both	all
anybody	everyone	one	few	any
anyone	much	nothing	many	more
anything	everything	somebody	several	most
each	neither	someone		none
either	nobody	something		some

Use a singular personal pronoun to refer to a singular indefinite pronoun. Use a plural personal pronoun to refer to a plural indefinite pronoun.

> <u>Everyone</u> has a right to cast <u>his</u> or <u>her</u> own vote. (singular)

> <u>Many</u> of the suffrage workers believed in <u>their</u> cause passionately. (plural)

Some indefinite pronouns can be singular or plural. Use the meaning of the sentence to determine whether the indefinite pronoun is singular or plural. If the indefinite pronoun refers to members of a group, use a plural personal pronoun.

> <u>Some</u> of the philosophy of the women's movement of the 1800s had <u>its</u> beginnings during the Age of Reason of the late 1700s. (singular)

> <u>Most</u> of the suffrage workers knew the risks <u>they</u> were taking. (plural)

Using Indefinite Pronouns

Choose the correct pronoun from those in parentheses.

1. Most of the women in the United States simply take for granted (her, their) right to vote.

2. However, during the mid-1800s, anyone who advocated granting voting rights to women risked (their, his or her) reputation as a sensible person.

3. Almost nobody thought (he or she, they) was being insensitive by saying that women were not intellectually or emotionally equipped to vote wisely.

4. Few of us would consider giving up (his or her, our) vote today, believing instead that voting is essential for full citizenship.

5. Susan B. Anthony was someone who felt that (their, her) rights were being ignored.

6. Anyone living in the United States today would not believe (his or her, their) eyes if they saw a woman arrested just for the crime of voting.

7. However, most of the country turned (their, its) back when that happened to Susan B. Anthony in 1872.

8. Anthony was fined $1,000 for voting illegally; she was proud to be one of the many who have suffered for (her, their) principles.

CHAPTER 8

Lesson 6

Indefinite Pronouns as Antecedents

More Practice

A. Identifying Indefinite Pronouns

Underline the indefinite pronoun in each sentence. Then underline the correct pronoun(s) in parentheses.

1. Each of the members of the chorus signed (their, his or her) name on the card.

2. Everyone put on (his or her, their) coat again and headed outside.

3. Many students want this job; several have sent us (his or her, their) applications.

4. Some of the perfume has lost (its, their) scent.

5. Most of this year's concert goers are renewing (his or her, their) memberships for next year.

6. Neither of the children could find (his, their) boots.

7. If anyone calls, tell (him or her, them) that I will be late.

8. Some of us bought (his or her, our) tickets several weeks ago.

9. Both of the printers had problems with (its, their) connections.

10. Both applicants are serious about helping; either would do (his or her, their) best.

11. If any of the glue leaked out of the bottle, (it, they) will be hard to clean up.

12. Everything was back in (its, their) place after the party.

B. Using Pronouns Correctly

In each sentence below, decide whether the pronouns agree with their antecedents. If the sentence is correct, write **Correct** on the line. If it contains a pronoun that does not agree with its antecedent, rewrite the sentence correctly on the line.

1. Will somebody please move their car from the driveway immediately?

_____

2. Just a few of the swimmers have their lifesaving certificates.

_____

3. If anyone has a copy of the book, they should pass it up to the front.

_____

4. Neither of the kittens can find their toy.

_____

5. All of the T-shirts had had their labels removed.

_____

6. Each of the club members signed their name on the petition.

_____

7. Neither of the new cars performed satisfactorily in their safety test.

_____

For use with Pupil's Edition pp. 191–193

CHAPTER 8

Lesson 6

Indefinite Pronouns as Antecedents

Application

A. Proofreading for Pronoun-Antecedent Errors

Proofread the following paragraph. When you find an error involving a pronoun and its agreement with its antecedent, cross the pronoun out. Then insert this proofreading symbol ʌ and write the correct pronoun or pronouns above it.

Elizabeth Cady Stanton was an early leader in the fight for women's rights. During the 1800s, everybody involved in the controversy surrounding women's rights had their own opinion about this unusual woman. While she was a fervent supporter of women's issues, she was also a devoted wife and mother. Each of her seven children knew that Stanton put their welfare ahead of her political philosophy. Even so, Stanton was fully involved in securing full citizenship for women for all of her adult life. Some of her beliefs were amazing for its audacity in a time when women were treated as property. She fought not only for women's right to vote, but also to own property themselves. Neither of these issues ever lost their importance to Stanton, who served the cause as president of the National Woman Suffrage Association for over 11 years. All of Stanton's efforts were justified when it resulted in the passage of the 19th Amendment to the Constitution—the one that granted women the right to vote.

B. Using Indefinite Pronouns in Writing

Write a brief biography of a family member or friend using at least four of these indefinite pronouns: *all, any, most, none, some*. Be sure that any personal pronouns agree with their indefinite-pronoun antecedents in number.

_____

_____

_____

_____

_____

_____

_____

_____

_____

CHAPTER 8

Lesson 7

Other Pronoun Problems

Reteaching

Pronouns may be used with an appositive, in an appositive, or in a comparison.

With an appositive An appositive is a noun or pronoun that follows another noun or pronoun to identify or explain it. The pronouns *we* and *us* are sometimes followed by appositives. The nominative case, *we*, is used when the pronoun is a subject. The objective case, *us*, is used when the pronoun is an object. To determine whether to use *we* or *us*, drop the appositive from the sentence, and determine whether the pronoun is a subject or an object.

> **We** <u>club members</u> held a membership drive. (<u>We</u> held a membership drive.)
> APPOSITIVE

> New students signed up with **us** <u>officers</u>. (New students signed up with <u>us</u>.)
> APPOSITIVE

In an appositive A pronoun used as an appositive is in the same case as the noun to which it refers.

> The project leaders, Jane and <u>she</u>, reported on their progress.
> (*Leaders* is the subject of *reported*; use the nominative case.)
> Audience members asked the project leaders, Jane and <u>her</u>, a few questions. (*Leaders* is the object of *asked*; use the objective case.)

In a comparison A comparison can be made using *than* or *as* to begin a clause. When words are left out of such a clause, the clause is said to be **elliptical**. To determine the correct pronoun to use in an elliptical clause, mentally fill in the unstated words.

> My brother is older than <u>I</u>. (am)

Choosing the Correct Pronoun

Underline the correct pronoun from the two given in parentheses.

1. (We, Us) neighbors are planning a neighborhood garden.
2. An official from the city told (we, us) residents to decide where we wanted the garden.
3. No one can make a speech as well as (he, him).
4. Our two leaders, Lila and (him, he), will speak at the next city council meeting.
5. We chose those two, Ernesto and (she, her), because they are comfortable speaking to large groups of people and are enthusiastic about the garden.
6. Lila is a faster thinker than (me, I).
7. Our council representatives, Mr. Conti and (she, her), are in favor of the idea.
8. We sent our petition to our representatives, Ms. Jackson and (he, him), so they would understand that the neighborhood supports the garden.
9. Mr. Conti is more knowledgeable about our neighborhood than (she, her).
10. The efficiency of the council impressed all of (we, us) observers.
11. Both representatives, Mr. Conti and (she, her), quickly voted for the resolution.
12. (We, Us) residents can now begin turning over the soil in our new garden.
13. Our representatives are as pleased with the results as (we, us).
14. The endeavor was a success for (we, us) would-be gardeners.

For use with Pupil's Edition pp. 194–196

CHAPTER 8

Lesson 7 **Other Pronoun Problems**   *More Practice*

A. Choosing the Correct Pronoun

Underline the correct pronoun of the two given in parentheses.

1. Robin is a better archer than (I, me).

2. (We, Us) actors practiced our lines backstage.

3. Betty wrote a better monologue than (he, him).

4. The candidates, Chris and (she, her), presented their platforms at the school assembly.

5. The prizes were awarded to the only remaining dancers, Julio and (her, she).

6. Do you think anyone sings as well as (her, she) today?

7. The librarian led (we, us) students to the correct shelf.

8. The last people in line, Deanne and (I, me), turned off the lights and closed the door.

9. In general, I believe you usually do a more thorough job than (they, them).

10. They are just as surprised as (we, us) about the new court ruling.

11. The coach and (we, us) swimmers will go to Florida on spring break.

12. The director of the competition distributed the rules to (we, us) contestants.

B. Using Pronouns Correctly

Write an appropriate pronoun on the line in each sentence. Do not use the pronoun *you* or any possessive pronouns.

1. Sue is interested in the subject, and I am just as interested in it as _____.

2. Lou can jump farther than _____.

3. I hope the judges agree than no one danced better than _____.

4. _____ citizens have a right and a responsibility to vote.

5. The two people who always waited at the bus stop, Bob and _____, became good friends.

6. I can't believe that anyone else is as hungry as _____!

7. An employee took orders from _____ diners as we waited in line for service.

8. Susan B. Anthony may be more well known than _____ now, but Elizabeth Cady Stanton was responsible for many of the ideas of the suffrage movement.

9. The police asked the victims, Peter and _____, for a full description of the suspects.

10. I wonder why you always seem to be colder than _____.

CHAPTER 8

Lesson 7

Other Pronoun Problems

Application

A. Writing Elliptical Sentences Using Pronouns

Write an elliptical sentence with the same meaning as each of the following sentences. Replace the boldfaced noun with a pronoun. Use the correct pronoun to communicate your meaning.

> **EXAMPLE** Liz can ride a bike faster than **Claire** can ride.
> *Liz can ride a bike faster than she.*

1. Liz is just as excited about the race as **Claire** is.

_____

2. For weeks, Liz has practiced more regularly than **Claire** has.

_____

3. Claire has been busier with school work than **Liz** has been.

_____

4. If you needed a partner in a race, would you have chosen Liz or would you have chosen **Claire?**

_____

5. It is obvious that Liz feels more invested in bicycling than **Claire** feels.

_____

6. Liz deserves to win the race more than **Claire** deserves to win.

_____

_____

B. Proofreading for Correct Pronoun Usage

Proofread the following paragraph. When you find a pronoun used incorrectly, cross it out. Then insert this proofreading symbol ∧ and write the correct pronoun above it.

    Us voters are faced with a difficult decision this fall. The candidates say

they have a more comprehensive view of the challenges and potential pitfalls

that face us than the normal citizen does. They tell us voters that they can see

the problems more clearly than us. I am sure that these candidates are no

less interested in the welfare of the city than we. However, us voters must

learn to think for ourselves and look beyond the rhetoric. The candidates, the

former mayor and the challenger, are letting we voters see and discuss only

their own agendas. We citizens must focus on the issues that we know are

important. In some ways, we are better informed than them because we are

not protected by wealth or privilege, as they are. When we voters debate the

issues, let us not be led into discussing bogus issues introduced by these

manipulative candidates, the mayor, and her.

(For use with Pupil's Edition pp. 194–196)

CHAPTER 8

Lesson 8 # Pronoun Reference   *Reteaching*

Avoid these pronoun reference problems.

Indefinite reference is a problem that occurs when the pronoun *it, you,* or *they* does not clearly refer to a specific antecedent. Eliminate this problem by rewriting the sentences in which the pronouns appear.

> **Awkward**   In the rule book, they say that coaching a partner is forbidden.
> **Revised**   The rule book states that coaching a partner is forbidden.

A **general reference** problem occurs when the pronoun *it, this, that, which,* or *such* is used to refer to a general idea rather than to a specific noun antecedent. Correct the problem by adding a clear antecedent or by rewriting the sentence without the pronoun.

> **Awkward**   You have been giving your partner hints, which gives you
>   an unfair advantage.
> **Revised**   Your habit of giving your partner hints has given you an
>   unfair advantage.

An **ambiguous reference** problem occurs whenever more than one word might be a pronoun's antecedent. Eliminate the problem by rewriting the sentence to clarify what the pronoun refers to.

> **Awkward**   Those players are not playing fair; she keeps giving her hints.
> **Revised**   Those players are not playing fair; Trish keeps giving Ann hints.

Identifying Clear Pronoun References

In each group of sentences below, one sentence has an indefinite, general, or ambiguous pronoun reference. The other is correct. Underline the one that is correct.

1. Gerald told Hal that the handwriting looked like his.
   Gerald told Hal that the handwriting looked like Hal's.

2. They said on the television news that a thunderstorm is coming.
   The TV weatherperson said that a thunderstorm is coming.

3. Because this summer has been dry, growing watermelons has been tricky.
   This has been a dry summer, which has made growing watermelons tricky.

4. On the score, it has the trombones resting for four measures.
   The score instructs the trombones to rest for four measures.

5. Like most of his friends, Sasha looks forward to pizza day at the cafeteria.
   Sasha looks forward to pizza day at the cafeteria. That is how most of his
   friends feel, too.

6. The photograph and the article appeared in today's paper; I know that because
   I saw it briefly.
   When I looked at today's paper briefly, I saw both the photograph and the article.

7. The ad states that milk provides essential nutrients such as calcium.
   In the ad, they say that milk provides essential nutrients such as calcium.

8. If they want us to recycle, they should provide us with clear rules.
   If the sanitation department wants us to recycle, officials should provide us
   with clear rules.

CHAPTER 8

Lesson 8

Pronoun Reference

More Practice

Avoiding Indefinite, General, and Ambiguous References

Rewrite the following sentences to correct indefinite, general, and ambiguous pronoun references. More than one interpretation may be possible. Add any words that are needed to make the meaning clear.

1. Using bones they have found, they are rebuilding the dinosaur.

_____

2. A finch egg is the size of a marble, and it weighs one gram.

_____

3. In the preface it explains how they used to live on homesteads in the 1800s.

_____

4. We removed the pictures from the walls and cleaned them thoroughly.

_____

5. Jessica took the turtle out of the terrarium and washed it.

_____

6. In the 19th century, you had to work 12-hour days.

_____

7. Brian understood the introduction to *The Scarlet Letter* after he read it.

_____

8. In some parts of the West, you get very little rainfall.

_____

9. Bill and Karen unloaded the bags from the shopping carts and returned them.

_____

10. It has been raining off and on for three days. This has made Gretchen appreciate sunny weather.

_____

11. Mike told Paul that he was the next player to bat.

_____

12. In the program, they list the graduates in alphabetical order.

_____

CHAPTER 8

For use with Pupil's Edition pp. 197–199

Pronoun Reference

Application

A. Eliminating Pronoun Reference Problem

Revise the sentences below to correct all indefinite, general, or ambiguous pronoun reference problems. More than one interpretation may be possible.

1. At the meeting, they introduced the teacher advisors for the club.

_____

2. The wizard Merlin told the young King Arthur that the sword was his.

_____

3. Michelle counts on her friends to take good notes, which is a good idea until your friends are absent one day.

_____

4. Lenny and his brother played catch while he ate a sandwich.

_____

5. In this magazine, you usually have a variety of articles by well-known authors.

_____

B. Using Clear Pronoun References

In the following paragraph, find five sentences with indefinite, general, or ambiguous pronoun references. Revise the sentences on the lines below.

(1) They often use Harlem as an example of urban poverty. **(2)** This section of New York City, however, once enjoyed better days. **(3)** African-American literature and culture flourished during the Harlem Renaissance of the 1920s. **(4)** Musicians from New Orleans brought jazz to Harlem. **(5)** Intellectuals flocked to Harlem circles because you had a stimulating atmosphere. **(6)** Writers and activists such as W. E. B. DuBois argued for full and immediate racial equality. **(7)** Poets such as Langston Hughes found it meaningful to write about black urban life. **(8)** As white readers sampled the work of Hughes, Claude McKay, and others, their reputations spread. **(9)** Its cultural contributions endured long after the Great Depression had caused economic decline in Harlem.

_____

_____

_____

_____

_____

_____

CHAPTER 9

Lesson 1

Using Adjectives and Adverbs

Reteaching

Modifiers are words that give information about, or modify, the meanings of other words. **Adjectives** modify nouns and pronouns. They answer the questions *which one* (this, those), *what kind* (powerful, lovely), *how many* (several, six), or *how much* (some, enough).

Words classified as other parts of speech also can be used as adjectives.

Nouns	<u>canoe</u> trip
Possessive Pronouns	<u>their</u> life jackets
Demonstrative Pronouns	<u>that</u> shore
Participles	<u>rising</u> waters, <u>broken</u> paddle
Indefinite Pronouns	<u>all</u> eels
Numbers	<u>18</u> hours

Most adjectives come before the words they modify. A **predicate adjective,** however, follows a linking verb and modifies the subject of a clause.

The river is <u>high</u>. (The adjective *high* modifies the noun *river*.)

Adverbs modify verbs, adjectives, and other adverbs. They answer the questions *where* (far, east), *when* (soon, later), *how* (quickly, warmly), or *to what extent* (quite, rather).

Modifies verb	The trip went <u>smoothly</u>.
Modifies adjective	We were <u>extremely</u> excited.
Modifies adverb	We left <u>very</u> early.

Identifying Adjectives and Adverbs

Identify the boldfaced word as an adjective or an adverb. Write **ADJ** or **ADV** on the line.

1. The river seemed **calm** and peaceful at the start of the canoe trip. _____

2. I **always** enjoy canoeing down a quiet river. _____

3. On this day, the wind was blowing rather **briskly.** _____

4. **Several** people were swimming in the river. _____

5. In our canoe, we carried a cooler filled with a **picnic** lunch. _____

6. We floated down the river **lazily** for about two hours. _____

7. We arrived at our lunch spot **later** than we had expected. _____

8. At last, we noticed that the sky was slowly becoming **gray,** not blue. _____

9. In addition, the wind was picking up and blowing even **stronger** than before. _____

10. We also noticed that there were **fewer** canoeists around now. _____

11. The sound of a **distant** rumble told us to hurry. _____

12. We became **slightly** nervous and started to paddle quicker. _____

13. While before we had paddled rather **carelessly,** now we were serious. _____

For use with Pupil's Edition pp. 208–210

Lesson 1

Using Adjectives and Adverbs

More Practice

A. Identifying Adjectives and the Words They Modify

Underline the adjective once and the word it modifies twice in each of the following sentences. Ignore articles and proper nouns.

1. The Mississippi River is an important waterway in the United States.
2. It has played a vital role in American history.
3. This mighty river starts small in northwestern Minnesota.
4. When the Minnesota River joins it, the Mississippi grows larger.
5. At least four other rivers flow into the Mississippi, and by the time it reaches the Gulf of Mexico, this river is impressive indeed.
6. Melting glaciers provided some of the river water after the Ice Age.
7. Many people enjoy traveling down the Mississippi on paddlewheel riverboats.
8. Strolling minstrels entertain them on this trip to the past.
9. Various industries use the Mississippi as a way to transport goods to foreign ports.
10. Goods are transferred to international ships in the busy port of New Orleans.

B. Identifying Adverbs and the Words They Modify

Underline the word modified by each boldfaced adverb. Then in the blank after each sentence, identify the part of speech of the modified word. Write **V** for verb, **ADJ** for adjective, or **ADV** for adverb.

The lion <u>defended</u> its cubs **ferociously.** ____V____

1. I feel **unbelievably** hungry after I swim. _____
2. Some German words **closely** resemble related words in English. _____
3. The carvings on the old chest were **quite** unusual. _____
4. John looked **intently** at the painting. _____
5. **Very** carefully, he pulled away the plastic cover. _____
6. I think that car is **ridiculously** expensive. _____
7. A mathematician must think **logically** to solve equations. _____
8. The waitress took our order **quickly** and disappeared into the kitchen. _____
9. The storm broke **quite** unexpectedly. _____
10. My car is **unbearably** hot after it sits in the sun all day. _____

Lesson 1

Using Adjectives and Adverbs   *Application*

A. Writing Subjects and Predicates

Complete each of the following sentences by writing an adjective or an adverb in the blank. Then write **ADJ** or **ADV** on the line to identify your word.

1. When you live on a river, flooding is _____ a danger.   _____

2. Although the river is _____, it is also dangerous.   _____

3. In the spring, _____ snow can swell a river beyond its banks.   _____

4. People living near the river must be _____.   _____

5. They must check the river levels _____ to make sure they are within safe limits.   _____

6. The river can rise _____ quickly after a few days of steady rain in the spring.   _____

B. Writing with Adjectives

On the lines below, write a description of a person you know well. Use at least six different adjectives in your description. Use a separate piece of paper if necessary.

_____

_____

_____

_____

_____

C. Writing with Adverbs

Imagine that you suddenly found out that you had won a million dollars. How would you feel? How would you act, speak, and move? On the lines below, describe the moment when you discover that you are a winner. Use at least six different adverbs in your description. Use a separate piece of paper if necessary.

_____

_____

_____

_____

_____

Lesson 2 Problems with Modifiers

Reteaching

In deciding whether to use an adverb or an adjective, follow these guidelines: Use an **adjective** if the word modifies a noun or pronoun. Use an **adverb** if the word modifies a verb, adjective, or another adverb.

Two pairs of words, *good* and *well* and *bad* and *badly*, can cause special problems. Study these models of correct uses.

good (adjective)	I feel <u>good</u> when I ride my bike.
well (adjective)	I didn't feel <u>well</u> yesterday, so I stayed in bed.
well (adverb)	He paints <u>well</u>.
bad (adjective)	I felt <u>bad</u> when I heard the news.
badly (adverb)	She sang <u>badly</u>.

Avoid using **double negatives**—two negatives in a clause. (Nonstandard: I *don't* have *no* pencil.) The words *hardly, barely,* and *scarcely* are considered negative.

This, that, these, and *those* are demonstrative pronouns used as adjectives. They must agree in number with the words they modify. *Here* and *there* are never used with demonstrative adjectives (Nonstandard: *this here* dog). *Them* is never used as an adjective in place of *these* or *those* (Nonstandard: *them* stars).

Using the Correct Modifier

Underline the correct word in parentheses in each sentence.

1. Karin stubbed her toe rather (bad, badly) when she tripped in the dark.
2. We got hardly (any, no) sleep on the train last night.
3. Your new employee seems (dependable, dependably).
4. The speaker stepped away from the podium because he didn't feel (good, well) enough to continue.
5. Watch the soup on the burner (closely, close), or it might boil over.
6. Those shoes look (real, really) comfortable.
7. Those scissors haven't cut (good, well) ever since you used them to cut sandpaper.
8. It was (lucky, luckily) that you found your key.
9. The colonists couldn't see (any, no) reason to pay the stamp tax.
10. What breed is (that, that there) dog?
11. I can't see (well, good) enough to read that sign in the window.
12. The young mother spoke (tender, tenderly) to her new baby.
13. Don't feel (bad, badly) that you lost the book; we'll buy a new one.
14. We had hardly (no, any) time to wait before the bus arrived.
15. The contestant felt (good, well) about her performance.
16. The striking employees claim that they have been treated (bad, badly) by management.
17. (These, This) type of computer has proven unreliable.
18. The voice on the phone sounded (frantic, frantically).

Lesson 2

Problems with Modifiers

More Practice

A. Using the Correct Modifier

Underline the correct word in parentheses in each sentence.

  1. (That, That there) fish is too small to keep.

  2. This job looks (easy, easily), but looks can be deceiving.

  3. Terri didn't ask for (no, any) help when she painted her bedroom.

  4. How (accurately, accurate) are the local weather forecasters?

  5. Luckily, this stream hasn't (ever, never) overflowed its banks.

  6. The assistant principal is used to handling (this, these) type of problem.

  7. Lightning flashed (wild, wildly) across the sky in a zigzag pattern.

  8. My dog's fur feels (soft, softly) when I pet him.

  9. I'd say your chances to win a scholarship are (good, well).

  10. I can't eat (them, those) french fries; they are too cold now.

B. Using Modifiers Correctly

Decide if modifiers are used correctly in the sentences below. If a modifier is used incorrectly in a sentence, rewrite the sentence correctly on the line. If the sentence is already correct, write **Correct** on the line.

  1. Mark feels good about himself when he does volunteer work.

  _____

  2. Because she didn't feel good, Maria played bad at her recital.

  _____

  _____

  3. Let's see if one of them computers over there is connected to the Internet.

  _____

  _____

  4. The rain hadn't scarcely begun when the game was called.

  _____

  _____

  5. This here movie star is one of my favorite actresses.

  _____

  _____

  6. My mother feels badly because she missed my performance.

  _____

  _____

For use with Pupil's Edition pp. 211–214

Lesson 2

Problems with Modifiers

Application

A. Using Adjectives and Adverbs Correctly

Write sentences in which you correctly use the adjectives and adverbs given.

1. real _____

2. really _____

3. bad _____

4. badly _____

5. good _____

6. well _____

7. hardly _____

8. scarcely _____

B. Writing with Adjectives and Adverbs

The following paragraph has seven errors involving modifiers. Identify the errors, and then write the paragraph correctly on the lines.

The recent music competition tested the skills of our school's musicians. All the participants had practiced for weeks and came ready to play as good as they could. Many of them were real nervous before they played for the judges. However, when they performed, most of them didn't show hardly any jitters. Only one participant played bad because she wasn't feeling good, and the judges were understanding. They seemed to feel bad for her and rated her higher than she probably deserved. In fact, them judges seemed to want all the contestants to do well. These kind of competitions are good for our music students because they give these developing musicians a goal to aspire to and a place to display their talent and dedication.

_____

_____

_____

_____

_____

_____

_____

_____

CHAPTER 9

Lesson 3

Using Comparisons

Reteaching

Modifiers can be used to compare two or more things. Use the **comparative** form of a modifier when comparing two persons, places, things, or actions. Use the **superlative** when comparing three or more.

Adjectives
Comparative   This computer is <u>faster</u> than that one.
Superlative   This is the <u>fastest</u> computer of all.

Adverbs
Comparative   The sun shines <u>brighter</u> than the moon.
Superlative   The sun seems to shine <u>brightest</u> of all heavenly bodies.

Most one-syllable and two-syllable words form the comparative by adding *-er*, and the superlative by adding *–est* (fast**er**, fast**est**). To form the comparative or superlative form of most modifiers with more than two syllables and modifiers that sound awkward with *-er* and *–est*, combine the regular form with the words *more* and *most* (**more** unusual, **most** unusual). To make a negative comparison, use *less* and *least* (**less** interesting, **least** interesting).

Some often-used modifiers have irregular comparative and superlative forms: *bad, worse, worst; good, better, best; well, better, best; ill, worse, worst; little, less or lesser, least; far, farther, farthest; many, more, most; much, more, most.*

A. Identifying Comparative and Superlative Modifiers

On the line, label the boldfaced modifier **C** for comparative or **S** for superlative.

1. Does the robin have **worse** sight than the eagle?   _____

2. To me, the **most fascinating** animal we saw at the wildlife park was the mountain lion.   _____

3. The **shortest** distance between two points is a straight line.   _____

4. My home computer performs **more reliably** than the one in class.   _____

5. Marina's costume for the party was original, and Theo's was very funny, but John's was **best** of all.   _____

B. Using Modifiers in Comparisons

Study the boldfaced modifier in each sentence. If the comparison is correct, write **Correct** on the line. If the comparison is incorrect, rewrite it correctly.

1. All of these paintings are beautiful, but the still life by Paul Cézanne appeals to me **most.**   _____

2. The photographs you took with this new camera are **sharpest** than the others.   _____

3. Do you feel **better** today than you felt last night?   _____

4. The church of Hagia Sophia in Istanbul is one of the **more spectacular** buildings in the world.   _____

For use with Pupil's Edition pp. 215–217

Lesson 3 # Using Comparisons

More Practice

Using Comparisons

Underline the correct form of comparison for each sentence.

1. Which planet has the (larger, largest) orbit, Pluto or Neptune?

2. Earth is far (smaller, smallest) than Jupiter.

3. The atmosphere on Venus is (less hospitable, least hospitable) to human life than that of Earth.

4. Now that space probes have supplied us with new information, we have begun to understand the solar system (better, best).

5. We now believe that the Milky Way galaxy is (older, oldest) than our solar system.

6. Powerful telescopes help scientists see (farther, farthest) into space than before.

7. The moon is Earth's (closer, closest) neighbor in space.

8. Some of the (tinier, tiniest) objects in space are comets.

9. When does the Northern Hemisphere experience the (shorter, shortest) day of the entire year?

10. In winter, the Northern Hemisphere receives the (fewer, fewest) hours of sunlight.

11. The day on which North America has the (less, least) sunlight is December 21, also called the winter solstice.

12. Which planet has the (more, most) satellites?

13. The rings around Saturn can be seen (more easily, most easily) with a telescope than with the naked eye.

14. To me, the (more exciting, most exciting) trip possible would be a voyage to another planet.

15. I would be (more interested, most interested) in visiting Mars than any other planet.

16. I feel (more strongly, most strongly) than ever that we should continue to explore space.

17. In fact, space exploration may be the (more important, most important) task of the 21st century.

B. Using Modifiers in Comparisons

Study the boldfaced modifier in each of the following sentences. If the comparison is correct, write **Correct** on the line. If the comparison is incorrect, rewrite it correctly.

1. In my opinion, the cardinal sings **most creatively** than the sparrow. _____

2. Of all the jockeys in this race, Eddie finishes first **more often.** _____

3. Which do you think is **most intelligent,** a horse or a dog? _____

4. Between those two renditions of "The Star-Spangled Banner," hers was **worst.** _____

5. I always seem to like the book version of a story **better** than the movie version. _____

Lesson 3

Using Comparisons

Application

A. Using Comparisons in Sentences

Write sentences comparing the following items by using the comparative or superlative form of the word in parentheses.

> **EXAMPLE** one star to all other stars (bright)
> *I wished on the brightest star in the sky.*

1. one costume compared to all the others at a party (bad)

_____

2. one vacation compared with another (exciting)

_____

3. one car compared to another (reliably)

_____

4. manuscript compared to all others (old)

_____

5. one dive compared to another at a competition (good)

_____

6. one meal compared to all others (delicious)

_____

B. Using Comparisons in Writing

Imagine that you are shopping for a bicycle or a used car. Write eight questions you would ask the salesperson who is trying to sell you a vehicle. In each question, use a comparative or superlative form of an adjective or adverb.

1. _____

2. _____

3. _____

4. _____

5. _____

6. _____

7. _____

8. _____

For use with Pupil's Edition pp. 215–217

Lesson 4 — Problems with Comparisons   *Reteaching*

Avoid these errors in using comparisons.

Double Comparisons Do not use both *-er* and *more* to form the comparative. Do not use both *-est* and *most* to form the superlative.

Nonstandard:	Mountain climbing is a **more riskier** sport than many others.
Standard:	Mountain climbing is a **riskier** sport than many others.

Illogical Comparisons Do not compare something to itself unintentionally or compare two unrelated things.

Illogical:	This mountain is taller than any mountain.
Clear:	This mountain is taller than any **other** mountain.
Confusing:	I like climbing better than my friend.
Clear:	I like climbing better than my friend **does.**

A. Using Comparisons Correctly

Choose and underline the correct modifier in each sentence.

1. Climbing the (highest, most highest) mountains is fun for some extreme athletes.
2. Climbing the big ones is much (more harder, harder) than regular climbing.
3. On the world's tallest mountains, you have a much (better, more better) chance of having a life-threatening accident.
4. The higher you climb, the (thinner, more thinner) the air gets.
5. The (leastest, least) exertion can exhaust climbers when their oxygen is low.
6. But perhaps avalanches pose the (worst, most worst) threat on a high mountain.
7. Even the (most skillfulest, most skillful) climber cannot outrun a sudden, unexpected avalanche.
8. Winds blow (more stronger, stronger) on high mountains than in the lowlands.
9. Wind in your face can make you move (slower, more slower) than normal.
10. Many adventurers say they feel (more alive, most alivest) on the highest mountains.

B. Using Comparisons Logically

In each pair of sentences, choose the sentence that uses modifiers logically and clearly. Underline that sentence.

EXAMPLE a.   I phone my mother more often than my aunt.
  b.   <u>I phone my mother more often than I phone my aunt.</u>

1. a. Extreme athletes are willing to take greater risks than any athletes.
   b. Extreme athletes are willing to take greater risks than any other athletes.
2. a. Some climbers have a greater love for the mountains than they have for their families.
   b. Some climbers have a greater love for the mountains than their families.
3. a. They think being in the mountains is better than being anywhere.
   b. They think being in the mountains is better than being anywhere else.
4. a. High mountain climbers may be more courageous than any other athletes.
   b. High mountain climbers may be more courageous than any athletes.

Lesson 4

Problems with Comparisons

More Practice

A. Using Comparisons Correctly

Choose and underline the correct modifier in each sentence.

1. Tony wore the (funniest, most funniest) costume to the party.
2. Elect the (most competent, most competentest) person to the office.
3. This room is (more colder, colder) than any other room in the house.
4. The red salsa is (spicier, more spicier) than the green salsa.
5. Whenever possible, I choose the (most brightest, brightest) colors available.

B. Correcting Double Comparisons and Illogical Comparisons

Rewrite each sentence to correct the incorrect, illogical, or confusing comparison.

1. Beth likes art class more than Ann.

_____

2. My friend Dave has more endurance than any swimmer I know.

_____

3. Of the two coins, the 1835 half-cent is most rarest.

_____

4. Ms. Pratt commutes as far, if not farther than, Mr. Ita does.

_____

5. Paul helped John more often than Mary.

_____

6. Kim enjoyed watching ballet more than Michelle.

_____

7. Miguel practices more hours than anyone on the team.

_____

8. Ms. Peng is the most busiest of the three counselors.

_____

9. The sun shines more often here than its does anywhere.

_____

10. Lynn remembers the star of that movie better than you.

_____

Lesson 4 — Problems with Comparisons

Application

A. Proofreading for Comparison Errors

The following paragraph contains several errors involving comparisons. When you find a modifier used incorrectly, cross it out. Then insert this proofreading symbol ∧ and write the correct modifier above it.

If you had to choose the most dangerous sport in the world, you would have to consider climbing frozen waterfalls. The risk-takers who try this sport see themselves as more braver than anyone. Perhaps they are simply more foolhardy than any athlete. The first step in ice climbing is finding an untouched waterfall hanging from a mountain cliff. To certain people, these giant icicles present a bigger challenge than anything they could encounter. They look at the waterfalls and say, "The more riskier, the better." Then they climb the waterfalls using an arsenal of special tools for digging into the ice. The dangers are real, and deadly falls are more commoner than they should be. Even so, ice climbers love their sport. Some climbers are willing to travel farther into the mountains to find a new waterfall than most people would consider sensible. They show themselves willing to put their lives on the line just to have some dangerous fun.

B. Using Comparisons in Writing

Imagine that you are a travel agent. You are describing various vacation resorts to a potential client. In doing so, you use at least five comparative and five superlative modifiers, either adjectives or adverbs. Write your sales pitch on the lines below.

_____

_____

_____

_____

_____

_____

_____

_____

_____

_____

CHAPTER 10

Lesson 1

People and Cultures

Reteaching

Capitalize these words and letters:

- people's names and initials that stand for names *Example:* Harry S. Truman
- people's titles and abbreviations of titles *Example:* Colonel Anderson, Col. Anderson
- abbreviations of some titles when they follow a name *Example:* William Frost, M.D.
- title used without a person's name if it refers to a head of state or a person in another important position *Example:* the Prime Minister
- title of royalty or nobility only when used with a person's name or in place of a person's name *Example:* Princess Margaret, the Princess
- title indicating family relationships only when used as part of name *Example:* Aunt Alice
- the pronoun *I*
- names of ethnic groups, races, languages, and nationalities, and the adjectives from those names *Example:* Asian American
- names of religions, religious denominations, sacred days, sacred writings, and deities *Examples:* Hinduism, Yom Kippur, Holy Spirit

Capitalizing Names of People and Cultures

Underline the letters that should be capitalized in each of the following sentences. If the sentence is already correct, write **Correct.**

1. george f. handel wrote operas and oratorios for the lutheran church. _____

2. His best-known work is *Messiah*, first performed before king george II centuries ago. _____

3. The king actually stood in awe when *The Hallelujah Chorus* was played. _____

4. Some say that handel's work marked the end of the dramatic and emotional Baroque Era of music. _____

5. Johann Sebastian Bach was a contemporary of Handel. _____

6. At an early age, bach began to study music with his father johann ambrosius bach, a town musician. _____

7. He learned the art of composition by copying the works of french, german, and italian composers. _____

8. My aunt harriet has a collection of bach's classical music. _____

9. Did you know that the famous composer Wolfgang Amadeus Mozart was a child prodigy? _____

10. Young mozart was an accomplished musician and composer by the age of six. _____

11. He became the official composer of the austrian court. _____

12. Unfortunately, mozart died at the early age of 35. _____

For use with Pupil's Edition pp. 228–230

Lesson 1

People and Cultures

More Practice

A. Capitalizing Names of People and Cultures

Underline the letters that should be capitals in each of the following sentences. If the sentence is already correct, write **Correct**.

1. German-born composer Richard Strauss composed symphonic poems for human voice. _____

2. Composer antonin dvorak from Czechoslovakia composed his symphony called *From the New World* on a visit to the United States. _____

3. For one of the movements of the piece, dvorak was inspired by an african-american spiritual called "Goin' Home." _____

4. Popular songwriter george gershwin wrote the musical comedy *Of Thee I Sing*, which won the Pulitzer Prize. _____

5. gershwin's *Rhapsody in Blue* inspired composers to use jazz formats in their writing. _____

6. Doing most of his work in the late 19th century, john philip sousa was known for his stirring marches. _____

7. i paraded with my uncle tim while the band played sousa's "Stars and Stripes Forever." _____

8. mayor pete bradshaw was the marshal of the parade that day. _____

9. Borrowing musical patterns from minstrel songs, scott joplin wrote such tunes as "Maple Leaf Rag." _____

10. Performers such as louis armstrong and jelly roll morton made jazz popular throughout American society during the 1920s. _____

11. Big band jazz was the style of duke ellington. _____

12. Our polish friends, lt. col. and mrs. wolinski, prefer the polkas they've come to love. _____

B. Capitalizing Correctly

Underline each lowercase letter that should be capitalized in the following paragraph.

(1) The history of Florida involves people from many countries and groups. (2) Native tribes such as the calusa and the tequesta lived in the area for thousands of years before europeans arrived. (3) In 1513, a spanish explorer became the first european to set foot in Florida. (4) Later, around 1564, a group of french colonists settled in what is now northern Florida. (5) However, they were driven out by the spaniards, who then ruled Florida for about 200 years. (6) Florida became an english possession after the French and Indian War. (7) Then, during the American Revolution, the english surrendered their land to spanish troops. (8) Finally, Florida came under american control during the War of 1812 when general andrew jackson seized Pensacola.

CHAPTER 10

Lesson 1

People and Cultures

Application

A. Proofreading

Proofread the following first draft of a report. Look especially for errors in capitalization. Draw three lines under each letter that should be capitalized. Draw a slash through any letter that is capitalized when it should be lowercase.

EXAMPLE <u>l</u>eonard <u>b</u>ernstein was an important <u>a</u>merican Ȼomposer.

Leonard bernstein was born in Lawrence, Massachusetts, in 1918. He studied the art of composition with walter piston and russian-born american conductor serge koussevitzky. leonard bernstein debuted as a conductor with the New York Philharmonic Symphony in 1943. He served as a professor at Brandeis University and at the Berkshire Music Center. Bernstein was a passionate composer, writing both Classical and Popular music. One of his most famous Works is *West Side Story*, a musical based on william shakespeare's play *romeo and juliet*. american and european audiences loved its Jazz Style and romantic story line. Although he himself was jewish, in 1971, Bernstein composed a beautiful work based on the roman catholic Mass. Bernstein's death in 1990 was a great loss for the international music community, but his work lives on.

B. Writing with Capital Letters

Suppose that you have been given the job of showing new students and their parents around your school. Write a short speech that you might give on your tour of the school. Include at least ten words that need capitalization, such as names of people, personal titles, family relationships, languages, and the pronoun *I*.

_____

_____

_____

_____

_____

_____

_____

_____

_____

_____

Lesson 2 # First Words and Titles *Reteaching*

Use capital letters to begin the following words:

- the first word of every sentence and of every line of traditional poetry
- the first word of a direct quotation, but not the first word of the second part of a divided quotation unless it starts a new sentence
- the first word of the greeting and of the closing of a letter
- the first word of each item in an outline and letters that introduce major subsection
- the first, last, and all other important words in titles; but not conjunctions, articles, or prepositions with fewer than five letters

Capitalizing First Words and Titles

Underline the words that should be capitalized in each of the following items. If the item is capitalized correctly, write **Correct** on the line.

1. the vet asked, "how did your dog get hurt?" _____

2. "ben is so friendly," his owner said, "that he ran into the street to say hello to me." _____

3. dear sir:
  this is to inform you that your order has arrived. you may pick it up
  at the warehouse any time during business hours.
        sincerely,
        John Stevens, Manager

4. I. poetry _____
    a. traditional
      1. form abcb
      2. ballad pattern
    b. modern

5. jim asked, "how much did your favorite movie, *the best years of my life*,
  make during its first year?" _____

6. On the television quiz show called *making a fortune*, players must think fast. _____

7. "Double, double, toil and trouble;
  Fire burn, and cauldron bubble." *William Shakespeare* _____

8. todd said, "i wonder if Bigfoot really exists." _____

9. we studied *the grapes of wrath* by John Steinbeck. _____

10. "there's a big shadow in the field," Al said. "it's from that hot-air balloon." _____

11. In our American history class, we studied the Declaration of Independence. _____

12. i have borrowed my brother's copy of *a tale of two cities*. _____

13. wallace Steven's poem "anecdote of the jar" is a modern
  American response to John Keats's "ode on a Grecian urn." _____

14. "Half the truth," Benjamin Franklin said, "is often a gentle lie." _____

For use with Pupil's Edition pp. 231–233

CHAPTER 10

First Words and Titles

More Practice

A. Capitalizing First Words and Titles

Underline the words that should be capitalized in the following sentences.

1. the 1965 Pulitzer Prize for literature went to Katherine Anne Porter for her *collected stories.*

2. As a young lifeguard in Dixon, Illinois, Ronald Reagan rescued 77 people from drowning.

3. "polar bears have black skin," commented our biology teacher Mr. Larrabee, "although their fur makes them look white."

4. following the tracks in the soft ground, we soon came upon an abandoned cabin.

5. "carrie, would you please bring me a glass of water?" asked Samantha. "i'm so thirsty."

6. because I could not stop for Death—
   he kindly stopped for me—   *Emily Dickinson*

7. "Come right this way, ladies and gentlemen," announced the master of ceremonies, "for the show of a lifetime."

8. "The man who does not read good books," said Mark Twain, "has no advantage over the man who can't read them."

9. Alfred, Lord Tennyson, wrote, "he makes no friend who never made a foe."

B. Capitalizing First Words in Letters

In the following letter, underline each word that has not been capitalized but should be.

dear Mom and Dad,

   my week here at Hartford College is going by quickly. it's been great to be with other writers my age. we read Mark Twain's "the celebrated jumping frog of calaveras county," and then we all wrote humorous short stories. I called mine "mr. piccolo's wonderful trip." i'll let you read it when I get home. maybe by then I'll know if it will be printed in the *Hartford summer Journal.*

love,

Lisa

C. Capitalizing First Words in Outlines

Underline each letter that should be capitalized in the following outline.

National Park System in California
  I. national parks
    a. sequoia
    b. yosemite
    c. death valley

  II. historic sites

First Words and Titles

Application

A. Writing a Letter

Write a letter to a network television producer to persuade her to keep your favorite programs on the air. Name four programs you like best and briefly explain why you like them. Include at least one imaginary quotation from a friend or family member who agrees with your opinion. Use traditional letter format. Be sure to capitalize correctly.

_____

_____

_____

_____

_____

_____

_____

_____

B. Writing an Outline Using Capital Letters Correctly

Read the following brief report. Then write a short outline for it on the lines below. Be sure to capitalize correctly.

The lions of Africa are magnificent animals. A mature lion will grow to between 350 and 400 pounds, while a grown female weighs in at about 250 to 300 pounds. From head to tail, males grow to a length of nine feet while females are about one foot shorter. Only males have the impressive manes that we all associate with the king of beasts.

Lions have almost legendary capabilities. They can jump 12 feet into the air and can run at speeds of 35 to 40 miles per hour. Perhaps the power of a lion is displayed most strongly in its roar, which can be heard up to five miles away.

Lions

_____

_____

_____

_____

_____

_____

_____

Lesson 3

Places and Transportation

Reteaching

Use capital letters to begin the following words connected with places and modes of transportation:

- each word in a geographical name except articles and prepositions
  Example: Rocky Mountains

- the words *north, south, east*, and *west* when they name a particular region of the country or world, or when they are part of a proper name *Example:* North Carolina

- names of planets and other specific objects in the universe (Do not capitalize *sun* and *moon.* Capitalize *earth* only when it refers to our planet or when it is used with other capitalized items. Never capitalize *earth* when it is preceded by the article *the* or when it refers to land surface, or soil.) *Example:* Earth (not the earth)

- names of specific buildings, bridges, monuments, and other landmarks
  Example: Independence Hall

- names of specific airplanes, trains, ships, cars, and spacecraft
  Example: USS Alabama

Capitalizing Names of Places and Transportation Modes

Underline the words that should be capitalized in each of the following sentences. If the item is capitalized correctly, write **Correct** on the line.

1. My family and I are planning a vacation to new york city. _____

2. We'll fly on a boeing 747 into la guardia international airport where my aunt and uncle will meet us. _____

3. New York City is located in the southeastern corner of New York State, across the river from New Jersey. _____

4. It actually consists of 50 small islands surrounded by the hudson river, the east river, and the new york bay. _____

5. Our hotel, the regency slumber inn, is at the south end of the brooklyn battery tunnel, in brooklyn, one of the five boroughs of new york. _____

6. brooklyn and queens are boroughs on the western end of long island. _____

7. The other boroughs are Brooklyn, Staten island, the Bronx, and Manhattan. _____

8. I hope we get to ride the staten island ferry, a double-ended boat that carries both people and cars across the harbor. _____

9. ellis island, where 16 million immigrants entered this country, now boasts a museum that is part of the statue of liberty national monument park. _____

10. The world trade center with its skyscraping twin towers is located in the heart of the financial district. _____

For use with Pupil's Edition pp. 234–236

Lesson 3

Places and Transportation

More Practice

A. Capitalizing Names of Places and Transportation Modes

Underline the words that should be capitalized in each of the following sentences.

1. From above, the great barrier reef looks like a watery great wall of china.

2. This buffer between australia's northeastern coast and the coral sea is a natural jewel; it adorns 12,500 miles of the queensland coastline.

3. The continent beyond is divided into three official regions: the eastern highlands, the central lowlands, and the western plateau.

4. Cities hug the rim, circling from northernmost darwin, west, south, and finally eastward up to sydney (named after the english statesman viscount sydney).

5. Explorers from holland wrote off this land as useless, but one englishman did not.

6. The land Captain James Cook "discovered" when he sailed the *endeavor* into botany bay in 1770 had already been inhabited for 50,000 years by natives.

7. The discovery was a bonus, for scientists on board had already fulfilled their goal, having stopped in tahiti to watch venus pass between earth and the sun.

8. The captain proceeded to name the bay for its rich plant life, to call the area new south wales, and to claim it for King George II and great britain.

9. In 1786, great britain decided to established a colony for convicted prisoners on new south wales.

10. When the governor and the convicts arrived, they found the bay too swampy, and their ships turned northward to sydney cove (now port jackson).

11. What started as a british convict colony became the nation's busiest port and a center of american-european trade and asian investment.

12. Its frontier spirit is reminiscent of our own west of many years ago.

13. Bold modern buildings such as the m.l.c. centre signal that brash optimism.

14. Since 1973, the sydney opera house, known for its sail-like roof, has attracted visitors from anchorage to zimbabwe.

15. Cook never found the northwest passage; instead, he opened up a new world.

B. Capitalizing Names of Places and Transportation Modes in a Paragraph

Underline each letter that should be capitalized in the following paragraph. Use a slash through any letter that is capitalized incorrectly.

Sun Festival Cruise Lines is proud to announce the debut of the *starlight empress*. Early next year, this beautiful new liner will embark for exotic destinations in the caribbean sea. The first port of entry will be on a beautiful island called martinique. We will then sail south to the undisturbed saint lucia, where white sandy beaches near the city of castries remain as beautiful today as they were when the French first landed on them in 1635. The water will appear even bluer as we head off to our next stops, the islands of antigua and saint kitts. Snorkeling and parasailing are popular sports in these modern paradise ports. The crystal clear caribbean sea holds adventure for you.

Lesson 3

Places and Transportation

Application

CHAPTER 10

A. Proofreading for Capital Letters

Read the following advertisement for a tour to a vacation spot. Draw three lines under any letters that should be capitalized but are not. Draw a slash through any letter that is capitalized incorrectly.

EXAMPLE I have always wanted to travel to <u>i</u>taly on the C̸oast of the <u>m</u>editerranean <u>s</u>ea.

Castle Tours has several highly coveted spots remaining on its Summer tour to italy. With the average temperature in July a comfortable 76 degrees, you'll find mountain climbing at brenner pass in the alps to be an exhilarating experience. A group will be guided up the highest Peak in italy, mont blanc, rising a majestic 15,000 feet above sea level. The second week of the tour will take you into two of the Country's most desired destinations. First, we'll board a lear jet and head toward romantic florence where the world of art awaits you. Imagine seeing the paintings of Raphael and Botticelli at the uffizi gallery. Then, on to medici chapel where the magnificent Michelangelo was both architect and sculptor. His spectacular Statue—*David*—originally created for the palazzo vecchio, can be seen at another gallery in the city. Your tour will end in Rome, the loveliest of italian cities. You'll toss three coins in trevi fountain, knowing all your dreams have come true on this vacation of a lifetime.

B. Using Capital Letters in Writing

Imagine that you are writing a travel article about a visit to your own town or city. Describe its location relative to other cities or geographical features, such as rivers or mountains. Describe its major attractions. Be sure to use at least one name from each of these categories: geographical names; geographical directions *north*, *south, east,* or *west*; monuments or landmarks; and, if possible, the name of an airplane, a train, or a ship. Use an additional piece of paper if necessary.

_____

_____

_____

_____

_____

_____

For use with Pupil's Edition pp. 234–236

Organizations and Other Subjects

Lesson 4

Reteaching

Use capital letters for the following:

- all important words in names of businesses, governmental agencies, institutions, and other organizations *Example:* United Appeal

- acronyms and abbreviations of the names of organizations and institutions *Example:* NASA (National Aeronautics and Space Administration)

- names of historical events, periods, and documents *Example:* the Cenozoic Era

- the abbreviations B.C., A.D., B.C.E., C.E., A.M., and P.M. (In typeset material, time abbreviations are usually shown as small capital letters. A.D. goes before the date; B.C. goes after it.)

- names of months, days, and holidays, but not names of seasons *Example:* Memorial Day, spring

- names of special events and awards *Example:* Nobel Prize

- brand names of products, but not a common noun that follows a brand name *Example:* High Bounce rubber balls

- name of a school course that is a language, contains a proper adjective, or is followed by a course number. (Do not capitalize the general names of school subjects) *Example:* French I, drafting

- the word *freshman, sophomore, junior,* or *senior* when used as a proper noun

Identifying Correct Capitalization

Underline the words or letters that should be capitals in each of the following sentences. If the sentence is correct, write **Correct.**

1. The university of iowa offers a good education and an exciting athletic program. _____

2. Do you know the name of our delegate to the united nations? _____

3. The Bill of Rights is the name of the first ten amendments to the Constitution. _____

4. On july 1, Canadians celebrate canada day, which until 1982 was called dominion day. _____

5. The conqueror alexander the great was born in 356 b.c. _____

6. The first oscar was bestowed in 1928. _____

7. We feed our parakeets bird banquet birdseed and no other brand. _____

8. The bureau of labor statistics publishes facts about United States workers. _____

9. The reformation was a religious movement of the 16th century. _____

10. On election day, the first tuesday after the first monday in november, the polls are open from 7:00 a.m. to 7:00 p.m. _____

Copyright © McDougal Littell Inc.

CHAPTER 10

Lesson 4

Organizations and Other Subjects   *More Practice*

A. Capitalizing Names of Organizations and Other Subjects

Underline each letter that should be capitalized in the following sentences.

1. The jurassic period is the second division of the mesozoic era.

2. Leaders in collective bargaining, the uaw has over a million members.

3. Nadia Comaneci set the standard for excellence when she won the gold medal at the 1976 montreal olympics.

4. The treaty of paris was signed on september 3, 1783, ending the american revolution.

5. The secretary ordered three cases of top-pro pens for the office staff.

6. Because I enjoy mathematics, I enrolled in algebra 2 as a sophomore.

7. Pope Leo II crowned Charlemagne emperor on Christmas Day, A.D. 800.

8. Col. Adam Winford was awarded the order of the purple heart posthumously for his bravery in the korean war.

B. Capitalizing Correctly

Underline the words in each sentence that should be capitalized. Then write them correctly on the corresponding lines below. If a sentence is capitalized correctly, write **Correct.**

(1) Students wishing to study aeronautical engineering have many options. **(2)** One of the leading schools to offer this program is the Massachusetts institute of technology. **(3)** Among its many special facilities, mit boasts five high-energy accelerators and a nuclear reactor on its premises. **(4)** Another university to consider is the alma mater of Neil Armstrong, purdue university. **(5)** Armstrong's colleague at the National Aeronaturics and Space Administration, Allen Bean, earned his degree at the university of texas. **(6)** Shortly after his graduation, he was chosen by nasa to be the chief of the skylab project. **(7)** Princeton University is the home of the james forrestal research center, world-renowned in aeronautical research. **(8)** With its close proximity to Cape Canaveral, Florida institute of technology, in Melbourne, Florida, has many advantages for the student interested in aeronautical engineering. **(9)** fit operates its own fleet of 50 planes and works cooperatively with scientists at the kennedy space center. **(10)** These schools and others are ready to provide seniors with their key to a future in flight.

1. _____   4. _____

2. _____   5. _____

3. _____   6. _____

7. _____   8. _____

9. _____   10. _____

Organizations and Other Subjects

Application

A. Proofreading for Capitalization Errors

Read the following speech given at the orientation meeting for new college students. Draw three lines under any letters that should be capitalized but are not. Draw a slash through any letter that is capitalized in error.

EXAMPLE The F̸aculty and staff of f̲airview u̲niversity say, "Welcome, f̲reshmen!"

As you begin your education at fairview university, we hope that you feel

the same Excitement and Anticipation that the faculty and staff are feeling.

When you enroll in your chosen courses, be they calculus 101 or german,

know that you can always count on the college to help you Succeed. If you

find yourself running into trouble, contact the student organization known as

stas, that is, student teacher association for success. There is, perhaps, in this

class, a future pulitzer prize winner, or a scientist, who will unlock Secrets of

the cenozoic era. Directly in front of me might be an inventor, like the alumnus

who created for the successful hi-tec computer company. Who knows what

the future holds? In june, four years from now, I hope to be addressing all of

you again at the fairview university commencement ceremony.

B. Using Capitalization in Writing

Imagine that you are raising money for a charitable organization. Write an advertisement aimed at potential donors explaining what your organization does. Explain that a meeting will be held and urge attendees to bring along one food item when they come. Be sure to use capital letters correctly in your ad. Include at least one of each of the following:

the name of the organization
a time abbreviation
a product's name

the name of a building
an award or special event
a day, date, or holiday

_____

_____

_____

_____

_____

_____

_____

For use with Pupil's Edition pp. 237–239

Lesson 1

Periods and Other End Marks

Reteaching

Use a **period** at the end of all declarative sentences, most imperative sentences, and most indirect questions.

Declarative sentence	Galileo was a scientist during the 17th century.
Imperative sentence	Describe Galileo's major contributions to science.
Indirect question	Galileo asked why people believed that the sun revolved around the earth.

Use a **period** after each number and letter in an outline or list.

Use a **period** at the end of these abbreviations. Examples are provided for each type.

Personal names	Titles		Business names	Addresses	
Robert E. Lee	Mrs.	Dr.	Corp.	St.	Blvd.

Chronology		Time of day		Measurement (English)	Time
A.D.	B.C.	A.M.	P.M.	3 ft. 5 in.	1 hr. 26 min.

Use a **question mark** at the end of an interrogative sentence or after a question that is not a complete sentence.

> What did Galileo see with his telescope? What else?

Use an **exclamation point** to end an exclamatory sentence, an imperative sentence that expresses strong emotion, or after a strong interjection.

> What a genius he was! Quick! Look up!

Using Periods and Other End Marks

Add periods, question marks, and exclamation points as necessary in the following items.

1. Where was Galileo born

2. Galileo's parents wanted him to become a doctor

3. Galileo, however, had no interest in medicine

4. Imagine Science history would have been so different if Galileo hadn't become interested in astronomy

5. When did Mr Jackson give his lecture about Galileo

6. As late as A D 1633, people generally believed that the sun and all the planets revolved around the earth

7. Years earlier, Polish astronomer Nicolaus Copernicus had proposed the theory that all the planets revolve around the sun

8. What made Galileo change his mind and accept Copernicus's theory

9. What courage it took to oppose the powerful Roman Catholic Church

10. During the Inquisition, Galileo was found guilty of publicly opposing church teachings

11. What was his punishment

12. Galileo was sentenced to live his life in isolation in a villa in Italy

13. What a waste of an excellent mind

For use with Pupil's Edition pp. 248–250

Lesson 1

Periods and Other End Marks

More Practice

A. Using End Marks

Add periods, exclamation points, and question marks where necessary in the following items. Draw a line through any period, exclamation point, or question mark that does not belong, and add the correct mark.

1. The invitation was addressed to Capt and Mrs David Scott

2. Dr Urban explained that tuberculosis was the leading cause of deaths in the United States in 1900

3. Hooray We've won the debate tournament

4. Have you ever studied ballet or modern dance!

5. How wonderful it is to meet you at last.

6. Entertainer Tom Thumb, whose real name was Charles S Stratton, grew to the height of only 3 ft 4 in

7. Ms B B Clough of Detroit, Michigan, won the grand prize

8. At 9:15 A M the satellite was launched

9. Katie asked if we had heard the latest weather bulletin

10. Would you like to go to dinner some evening next week

11. I   Galileo's early scientific endeavors
    A Tutored mathematics
    B Invented the hydrostatic balance
    C Taught at University of Pisa

12. In my opinion, this building is too cold And your opinion

13. Wait Don't you see that car coming!

14. The cabin attendant asked if I wanted a pillow and blanket?

15. Whew. What a long day it's been

B. Using End Marks in Writing

Add periods, question marks, and exclamation points where necessary in the following paragraph.

   (1) Ptolemy was one of the earliest astronomers **(2)** Although not much is known about him, we believe he was born around A D 100 in Alexandria, Egypt **(3)** What was his most influential theory **(4)** He decided that the earth was motionless in space and the moon, sun, and planets revolved around it **(5)** He asked why the stars behaved differently from the planets **(6)** The stars, he decided, were distant points of light attached to the inside of a giant rotating sphere **(7)** How different his theories were from those of modern-day astronomers **(8)** Even though his theories were eventually disproved, we need to give Ptolemy credit **(9)** How difficult it must have been to make calculations and observations with his primitive instruments

Periods and Other End Marks

Lesson 1

Application

A. Proofreading

Add periods, question marks, and exclamation points where necessary in the following paragraph.

Achoo Have you ever wondered where sneezes come from Sneezing is a sudden and violent rush of air through the nose and mouth A person has no control over it The body creates a sneeze to get rid of irritating objects in the nose You might ask why bright sunlight can also cause sneezing This is because the eye nerves are closely connected with nerve endings in the nose

According to Dr Murray A Gordon, Jr, of Oklahoma's Grant Hospital, "The way you sneeze is probably hereditary." A common inherited pattern is the "double sneeze," in which two sneezes occur just a few seconds apart Babies only a few weeks old have been known to sneeze in family patterns Although you can watch others sneeze, you can't watch yourself Have you ever noticed that it's impossible to sneeze with your eyes open If you want to know how you look when you sneeze, watch your parents

B. Using End Marks in an Outline

Think about your plans for the future, specifically your short-term goals and your long-term goals. Outline your future goals on the form below. Give the outline a title, and identify the two major divisions (short-term and long-term goals), and then supply three main ideas under each division. Be sure to punctuate correctly.

Title:

I _____

   A _____

   B _____

   C _____

II _____

   A _____

   B _____

   C _____

Comma Uses

Use **commas** after *first, second*, and so on when they introduce a series. Use **commas** between two or more adjectives of equal rank that modify the same noun. In a series of three or more, use a **comma** after every item in the series except the last one.

> When packing for a long hike, follow these steps: first, pack comfortable, easy-care clothing; second, pack toiletries such as soap, shampoo, and suntan lotion; and third, include any first-aid supplies or medicines you may need.

Use **commas** after introductory words or mild interjections such as *oh, yes, no,* and *well;* after an introductory prepositional phrase that contains additional prepositional phrases; and after verbal phrases, adverb clauses, and adverbs used as introductory elements.

> Yes, it's important to plan the trip carefully.
>
> In an emergency in the forest, these items will come in handy.
>
> When you're out on the trail, you'll appreciate the extra time you took to pack.

Use **commas** to set off words of direct address, such as names, titles, terms of respect, and phrases used to address an individual directly. Use **commas** to set off one or more words that interrupt the flow of thought in a sentence.

> Tina, you are ready, or so it seems, to begin your trek.

Use **commas** to set off these nonessential elements: clauses, participial phrases, and appositives.

> This trail, which my brother walked last year, will be difficult.
> My partner, interested in photography, is taking along two cameras.
> My favorite sport, hiking, is both inexpensive and fun.

Using Commas Correctly

Insert commas where necessary in the following sentences.

1. We toured the gardens in the following sequence: first the herb garden; second the lily pond; third the camellia garden; fourth the rose garden.

2. We learned that the oil in the jojoba plant is used in food preparation in lubricants for automobiles and in cosmetics.

3. Prickly pear cacti have flattened padlike stems.

4. While walking through the garden we were awed by the size of the eucalyptus trees the beauty of the water lilies and the agelessness of the yuccas.

5. Yes we enjoyed the different kinds of cacti.

6. Helen have you ever seen such a tall dangerous-looking cactus before?

7. This garden one of the oldest in the state is maintained by the local botanical club.

8. That herb which has been used in medicines for years grows well in this climate.

9. We decided at least I did that we would begin a garden at home.

10. The blossoms of the camellia may be red white pink or spotted with color.

11. We decided that these were the things we liked best in the garden: first the sweetbriar roses; second the golden barrel cactus; third the red camellias.

Comma Uses

More Practice

A. Using Commas

Underline the words in each sentence that should be followed by a comma. If no commas are necessary, write **None** on the line.

1. My favorite outdoor activities are hiking skiing and swimming. _____

2. At the end of this rugged steep trail you will get a great view of the valley below. _____

3. Michael can you read that trail marker? _____

4. The Appalachian Trail if I'm not mistaken extends almost 2,000 miles. _____

5. Naturally I would like to hike that trail sometime in my life. _____

6. The places I plan to hike are the following: first the Appalachian Trail; second a mountain trail in the Alps; third the trail to the Mount Everest base camp in Nepal. _____

7. Well I suppose I need to get into better shape for any of those treks. _____

8. While I see beautiful scenery I will be increasing my lung capacity and strengthening my leg muscles. _____

9. Planning my next trip will take time I'm sure. _____

10. My friend Chris who has already hiked in this area will come along on the trip. _____

11. By the time we return from our hike I will be in even better shape _____

12. What I experience on the trail will give me more confidence. _____

B. Using Commas in Writing

Insert commas where they are needed in the following paragraphs.

Many novels have been made into movies. The film *The Grapes of Wrath* was based on the novel by John Steinbeck. The story centers on an Oklahoma family named the Joads. They lose their home by bank foreclosure in the 1930s pack up their meager belongings and migrate to California to start a new life. The film starred Henry Fonda Jane Darwell and John Carradine. The talented creative actors worked together to convey a feeling of compassion for the poor.

Oliver! was a musical based on Charles Dickens's novel *Oliver Twist*. The fantastic choreography lively music and spectacular setting made this movie a memorable one. The songs "Consider Yourself" and "Food, Glorious Food" remain popular.

For use with Pupil's Edition pp. 251–254

Lesson 2 Comma Uses

Application

A. Writing with Commas

Add commas where they are needed in the following paragraph.

      Hiking is a sport that can be enjoyed by almost anyone. It is healthy inexpensive and fun. What are some basic rules of hiking? Well safe hiking demands that you do the following: first build up your endurance before you begin a long difficult hike; second take along necessary first aid and medical supplies; third never hike alone in the wilderness no matter how confident you feel. Of course just walking around your neighborhood is a good way to get into shape. One more advanced kind of hiking orienteering requires skills in map reading using a compass and traversing unfamiliar territory. A related sport that hikers enjoy is mountaineering. Mountain treks which should be attempted by only the most experienced of hikers can be difficult and dangerous. Even taking the danger into account it is clear that hiking is a sport you should consider trying.

B. Using Commas in Writing

Rewrite the sentences by following the directions in parentheses.

1. They packed the picnic basket. (Include a series of items.)

_____

2. This was going to be a feast. (Include two adjectives of equal rank that modify the same noun.)

_____

3. When they planned the menu, they considered three factors: nutrition; the expense of the food; the preferences of the guests. (Include *first, second,* and *third* to introduce a series.)

_____

_____

4. The picnic was a success for a number of reasons. (Include a series of reasons.)

_____

_____

5. The guests had a wonderful time. (Include a nonessential clause.)

_____

_____

CHAPTER 11

Lesson 3

More Comma Uses

Reteaching

Use **commas** to set off the explanatory words of a direct quotation, such as *she* said.

"Tell me more," she said, "about Native American tribes."

Use a **comma** before the coordinating conjunction that joins the two independent clauses of a compound sentence.

Columbus thought he had reached the Indies, and he called the native people he met here *Indians*.

Use a **comma** to separate words or phrases that might be mistakenly joined when they are read.

While hunting, Indians crossed the Bering Strait into North America.

Use **commas** to indicate the words left out of a parallel word group, or word groups that repeat the same structure.

The Cree lived in bark tepees; the Chippewa, in domed lodges.

Use a **comma** after the salutation of a friendly letter and after its closing.

Use a **comma** between the day of the month and the year (and after the year in a sentence); between the name of a city or town and state, province, or country, and after the state, province, or country; between a personal name and an abbreviation that follows it and after the abbreviation in a sentence; and after each item of an address (but not before or after the ZIP code). Use a **comma** after every third digit from the right in numbers of more than three digits. ZIP codes, phone numbers, years, and house numbers are exceptions to this rule.

Finally, use **commas** to avoid confusion before the conjunction *but* or *for* when it may be mistaken for a preposition; after an introductory adverb that could be mistaken for a prepositon; to separate a short introductory verbal phrase from the noun that follows it; and to separate repeated words.

Using Commas Correctly

Insert commas where necessary in the following sentences.

1. Dear Uncle Simon

   I am wrapping up a history project this year about Native-American tribes yet I still need some information. Can you tell me anything about the tribes that lived in your area of the country?

   Your nephew

2. Linda asked "How were the Indians able to cross the Bering Strait?"

3. Some experts believe the Indians settled in the Americas about 35000 years ago.

4. On February 18 1999 Dr. Calderon gave a lecture about the history of Native Americans in New Mexico.

5. Dr. Daniel Calderon Jr. returned recently to Albuquerque New Mexico where he had grown up.

6. The Plains tribes ate a great deal of meat but the tribes who lived on the coasts enjoyed a diet of fish and seafood.

For use with Pupil's Edition pp. 255–258

Lesson 3 — More Comma Uses

More Practice

A. Using Commas Correctly

Add commas where necessary in the following sentences.

1. The tornado ripped through the city yet no one was injured.
2. I gave Nicole the money and she gave me the ticket for the performance.
3. "Today" said Police Chief White "is a great day for the police academy."
4. The Battle of Gettysburg was fought from July 1 through July 3 1863 outside Gettysburg Pennsylvania.
5. "Knowledge may give weight but accomplishments give luster" wrote Lord Chesterfield "and many more people see than weigh."
6. On the spaghetti sauce and cheese were heaped.
7. The house at 35 Beale Street Brookline Massachusetts is John F. Kennedy's birthplace.
8. Betty Hoskins Ph.D. conducts nutrition research for Snacks Unlimited Inc.
9. The interior temperature of a star can be as high as 1100000 degrees C.
10. Katerina won a gold medal; Debi a bronze.
11. Maria asked for she was the only one who spoke Greek.
12. Was Martin Luther King Jr. assassinated in July 1968?
13. Before we lived at 12436 South Princeton Street.
14. Dear Joe Enclosed is the catalog I was telling you about. Your friend Diego
15. The information operator for ZIP code 02114 received 5200 calls last month.

B. Using the Comma in Paragraphs

Add commas where they are necessary in the following paragraphs.

On February 14 1994 I bought my first antique marble. Now I'm an avid collector. Anyone who likes collecting marbles should consider joining the Marble Collectors Society of America. There are about 3000 members. With your membership you receive a set of pictures illustrating 380 different marbles a newsletter that tells of auctions and marble fairs and a pricing guide. The Marble Collectors Society has set up good exhibits of marbles at the Corning Glass Museum in Corning New York; and the Smithsonian Institution in Washington D.C.

The prices of marbles have gone up dramatically in the last several years. In 1978 sulphides those with figures or portraits inside sold for $50 to $110. Now they go for $300 to $2000. To buyers high prices bring frowns; low prices smiles. Antique marble collecting is enjoyable and it can also be profitable.

CHAPTER 11

Lesson 3 — More Comma Uses

Application

A. Proofreading for Comma Usage

Insert this proofreading symbol ⋀ to add commas where they are needed. Use this proofreading symbol for deletion ⟋ , and cross out any commas that are not necessary.

The Pony Express was a mail-delivery service, that operated between St. Joseph Missouri and Sacramento California. It began its first run on April 3 1860. Its relays of men riding ponies carried letters, across a trail 1966 miles (3164 kilometers) long.

It usually took the Pony Express about ten days to make the run between St. Joseph and Sacramento. The fastest run occurred in March, 1861. A copy of an address to Congress by Abraham Lincoln President of the United States was delivered in seven and one-half days.

The transcontinental telegraph, opened on October 24 1861. In short delivery by the Pony Express was no longer the fastest means of communicating with the West. The Pony Express closed two days later. Its investors lost over $100000.

These days there are many successors to the Pony Express and the telegraph. The U.S. Postal Service and several private companies offer "fast-mail" deliveries. For example, a letter or package sent late in the afternoon of one day from Atlanta Georgia may be delivered to an address in Seattle Washington the next morning; or to an address overseas the morning after that. Radio TV the telephone and the computer of course are even more impressive. From one place to another anywhere on the earth they can communicate information instantaneously.

B. Writing with Commas

As you know, bands travel all over the country to give concerts in many cities. Write an imaginary conversation between members of a musical group, discussing their upcoming national tour. Include the names of cities, dates, and numbers above 999. Also include at least one compound sentence. Be sure that you use commas to avoid any reader confusion about your intended meaning. Remember to use commas correctly in direct quotations. Use a separate piece of paper if necessary.

_____

_____

_____

_____

_____

_____

_____

For use with Pupil's Edition pp. 255–258

Semicolons and Colons

Reteaching

Use a **semicolon** in the following ways: to separate items in a series if any of the items contain commas; to separate the independent clauses joined by a conjunction if either clause already contains commas; to join the independent clauses of a compound sentence if no coordinating conjunction is used; and before a conjunctive adverb, or a parenthetical expression, that joins the clauses of a compound sentence.

> Dams prevent flooding; provide power to cities, towns, and factories; and supply irrigation water to farms.

> Hoover Dam, one of the highest dams in the world, was completed in 1936; but it had been envisioned much earlier.

> Hoover Dam was built on the Colorado River; Lake Mead is its reservoir.
> It is important to the well-being of the West; in fact, it supplies water all the way to the Pacific Northwest.

Use a **colon** in the following ways: to introduce a list of items; between two independent clauses when the second clause explains or summarizes the first; and to introduce a long or formal quotation.

> The following dams are also located in the United States: Grand Coulee Dam, Shasta Dam, and Glen Canyon Dam.

> The need for a dam was apparent: the Colorado flooded in the spring and dried to a trickle during the summer.

> A local farmer wrote: "It's impossible to farm seriously when you cannot be confident of a steady supply of water for your crops. This situation is intolerable for farmers."

Also use a **colon** as in these examples:

> Dear Mr. Rogers: 6:15 a.m. Warning: Fire Hazard Genesis 6:9

Do not use a colon after a verb, in the middle of a prepositional phrase, or after *because* or *as*.

Using the Semicolon and Colon

Add the necessary semicolons and colons to the following sentences.

1. The dam consists of three parts the dam itself, the hydroelectric power plant, and the reservoir.

2. Residents felt the dam was desirable in fact, they thought it was essential.

3. Power generated by Hoover Dam is sent to Los Angeles, California Phoenix, Arizona and Las Vegas, Nevada.

4. The dam was named for President Hoover he was in office when it was begun.

5. It was officially named Hoover Dam in 1931 however, government departments began to call it Boulder Dam after Hoover left office.

6. Hoover Dam has been called Hoover Dam, Boulder Dam, and Boulder Canyon Dam but it has performed its job effectively, no matter what it has been called.

7. Hoover Dam is 725 feet high it is 1,244 feet long.

8. Caution There is a dangerous undertow near the dam.

9. We reached Hoover Dam at 3 30 P.M. and went on the last tour of the day.

Lesson 4

Semicolons and Colons

More Practice

A. Using the Semicolon and the Colon

On the lines, write the word from each sentence that should be followed by a
semicolon or colon. Then write the correct punctuation mark that should follow the
word. If a semicolon or colon is needed within a numeral, write the entire numeral
plus punctuation.

1. On February 25, 1986, Corazon Aquino became the President
   of the Philippines Ferdinand Marcos had resigned the
   presidency and fled the country. _____

2. China has the world's largest population however, the
   government strongly promotes a policy of one child per family. _____

3. It was Virginia Woolf who wrote these words "Anonymous
   was a woman." _____

4. My train for school leaves at 6 55 A.M. and arrives at 7 50 A.M. _____

5. The capital of California, the most highly populated state, is
   Sacramento and San Francisco and Los Angeles are
   California's most famous cities. _____

6. To Whom It May Concern   I am writing to request a refund. _____

7. Postal workers deliver mail in all types of weather rain,
   sleet, snow, and hail. _____

8. Bruges, Belgium, has long been famous for its lace in fact,
   it is one of the few places in Belgium where lace is still
   made by hand. _____

9. Take all the rain gear we expect bad weather. _____

B. Using the Semicolon and the Colon in Writing

Add semicolons and colons where they are needed in these paragraphs.

   (1) Frostbite is dangerous the skin and tissue can actually freeze as a
result of exposure to intense cold. **(2)** Frostbite can occur in many parts of
the body it most often affects the ears, nose, fingers, and toes.
   (3) In the early stages of frostbite, the skin appears red pain is often
present. **(4)** As the condition develops, the following symptoms appear skin
turns gray-white and the pain disappears at this stage the condition is easy to
treat. **(5)** A person who has frostbitten hands should cover the exposed area
with warm gloves then he or she should get out of the cold. **(6)** When the
person is indoors, he or she should follow these rules remove all wet clothing,
immerse the area in warm water, and cover the affected area loosely with dry
clothes. **(7)** Warning The person should not warm the frostbitten area by
sitting near a flame or radiator this heat might burn the skin.

For use with Pupil's Edition pp. 259–261

Lesson 4 — Semicolons and Colons

Application

A. Writing Sentences with Semicolons and Colons

For each item, write the sentence that is described in parentheses.

> **EXAMPLE** (sentence that uses a semicolon to join the parts of a compound
> sentence without a coordinating conjunction)
> *The plane was flying into a headwind; we arrived at the airport
> ten minutes behind schedule.*

1. (sentence that uses a semicolon before a conjunctive adverb and a comma to
   join clauses in a compound sentence)

   _____

   _____

2. (sentence that uses a colon to introduce a long quotation)

   _____

   _____

3. (sentence that uses a colon to introduce a list of items)

   _____

4. (sentence that uses a semicolon to separate parts when commas appear
   within parts of a series)

   _____

B. Proofreading a News Article

The reporter who wrote this news article was in a great hurry. He omitted both
semicolons and colons. Prepare the article for publishing by adding needed
semicolons and colons.

Fire engines responded to a fire in a warehouse in the northwest part of
the city, specifically the 1600 block of Lake Avenue, early this morning they
found the blaze out of control upon their arrival. Immediately they took these
precautions they kept gawkers far from the flames, they began hosing down
the building, and they called the owner. This fact was ascertained earlier no
one was in the building. The fire department called the departments of
neighboring cities however, the blaze was uncontrollable despite the efforts of
all the firefighters. Damages were said to be severe at least one million dollars'
worth of merchandise had been stored in the building. Fire investigators will
examine the site today they will look for signs of possible arson.

CHAPTER 11

Dashes and Parentheses

Reteaching

Use a **dash** to show an abrupt break in thought. If the thought continues after the break, **use a second dash.**

> Last Wednesday—a beautiful day—we visited the art museum.

Use **dashes** to set off a long explanatory statement that interrupts the main thought of the sentence.

> his painting—a landscape showing sun-drenched white buildings on a mountainside—is quite famous.

Use a **dash** to set off an introductory list.

> Strawberries, peaches, grapes—I put all these fruits in the salad.

Use **parentheses** to set off nonessential explanatory material that is loosely related to the sentence.

> he traffic (it was terrible!) kept us from arriving on time.
> This class is outstanding. (Three nationally-recognized scholars are guest speakers.)
> The train (an old steam engine) pulled out of the station.

Use **parentheses** to enclose numbers or letters in a list that is part of a sentence.

> The coach told us to (1) swim ten laps, (2) tread water for three minutes, and (3) get in line by the diving board.

In a research paper, use **parentheses** to identify the source of any quoted or paraphrased information you use.

> "The Greeks thought the world was managed by a multitude of beings, like another human world in general, but consisting of beings who had different powers from men." (Rouse, x).

Using Dashes and Parentheses

Insert dashes and parentheses where they belong in the following sentences.

1. That vacation I'll give you details later was unbelievable!
2. Underline and identify 1 the subject, 2 the verb, and 3 the complement.
3. I'm sure aren't you? that Marcia will get the job.
4. Andie can't practice her favorite sports skiing, tennis, and golf because of an injury.
5. Giant pandas, peregrine falcons, and Bali leopards these are endangered species.
6. "There is a new spirit abroad among women today" Miller, ix.
7. Lou Gehrig 1903–1941 set the record for consecutive games played.
8. First, let me show you oh, you already know how!
9. The word *funambulist* tightrope walker has a Latin derivation.
10. Measles, mumps, and whooping cough common childhood illnesses 50 years ago are now controlled by immunization.
11. *Uncle Tom's Cabin* the book that has often been linked with strong abolitionist feelings before the Civil War was written by Harriet Beecher Stowe.
12. The whale he was so huge! suddenly emerged in front of the ship.

For use with Pupil's Edition pp. 262–264

Lesson 5
Dashes and Parentheses

More Practice

A. Using the Dash in Sentences

Rewrite each sentence inserting dashes where they belong. Note that a dash (—)
is longer than a hyphen (-).

1. Solids, liquids, and gases we worked with all three in chemistry class.

_____

2. The book ends with no, you should read the ending yourself.

_____

3. This waterfall the longest in the world has been seen by only a few.

_____

4. The Pueblos their name came from a Spanish word meaning "village" live in
the Southwest.

_____

5. Buteos, kites, falcons all more commonly called hawks frequent our region.

_____

6. That director perhaps best known for his thrillers is respected around the world.

_____

B. Using Parentheses in Sentences

Rewrite each sentence, inserting parentheses where appropriate.

1. In his book, the senator advises against "unnecessary interference from the
executive branch" Tolland, 589.

_____

2. After our meeting, we decided to 1 call the custodian about reserving the
auditorium, 2 form a publicity committee, and 3 contact key local residents.

_____

3. Ohio its nickname is the Buckeye State joined the Union in 1803.

_____

4. Blue Canyon, California get the snow shovel out! is the snowiest town in the
United States.

_____

5. Prospect Creek, Alaska, recorded the coldest temperature in U.S. weather
history –80 degrees Fahrenheit.

_____

6. The Republican Party sometimes called the Grand Old Party was founded in 1854.

_____

CHAPTER 11

Lesson 5 Dashes and Parentheses   *Application*

A. Writing with Dashes and Parentheses

Rewrite the following sentences, inserting a word, phrase, or sentence set off by dashes or parentheses.

1. They are awarding first prize to Megan.

_____

2. This salad is delicious.

_____

3. Kris said, "Can you lend me a dollar?"

_____

4. The U.S. basketball team competed internationally.

_____

5. Abraham Lincoln spoke in a high-pitched voice.

_____

B. Writing with Dashes and Parentheses

Follow the directions to write and punctuate sentences correctly.

1. Write a sentence that uses a dash to show an abrupt break in thought.

_____

_____

2. Write a sentence that uses parentheses in a fragment within another sentence.

_____

_____

3. Write a sentence that uses a dash to set off an introductory list.

_____

_____

4. Write a sentence that uses parentheses to set off a complete sentence within another sentence.

_____

_____

5. Write a sentence that uses parentheses to enclose numbers or letters in a list that is part of a sentence.

_____

_____

For use with Pupil's Edition pp. 262–264

Lesson 6 — Hyphens and Apostrophes *Reteaching*

Here are ways to use the hyphen and the apostrophe.

Hyphens Use a hyphen in the following places:

- in compound numbers from twenty-one to ninety-nine;
- in spelled-out fractions, for example, *one-third;*
- in certain compound nouns, such as *mother-in-law, great-grandson;*
- in compound adjectives used before (but not after) a noun, such as *best-loved;*
- in words with the prefixes *ex-, self-, great-, half-,* and *all-* and all prefixes used before proper nouns and proper adjectives, such as *pre-Korean War;*
- with the suffixes *-elect* and *-style,* for example, *treasurer-elect;*
- when part of a word must be carried over from one line to the next.

Apostrophes Use an apostrophe in the following places.

- To form the possessive of a singular noun or an indefinite pronoun, add an apostrophe and an *s,* for example, *one sailor's cap* and *somebody's cap.*
- To form the possessive of a plural noun that ends in *s* or *es,* add only an apostrophe after the final *s,* for example, *two sailors' caps.*
- To form the possessive of a plural noun that does not end in *s,* add an apostrophe and an *s,* for example, *women's rights.*
- To form the possessive of a name that is difficult to pronounce when an apostrophe and an *s* are added, add the apostrophe alone, for example, *Euripedes' poems.*
- If the names of two or more persons are used to show joint ownership, have the last name show possession, for example, *Roberto and Kim's project.*
- If the names of two or more persons are used to show separate ownership, give each name the possessive form, for example, *Roberto's and Kim's reports.*
- Use an apostrophe with an *s* to form the plurals of letters, numerals, and words used as words, for example, *A's, 10's, no's.*
- Use an apostrophe in a date to show the omission of numbers, for example, *winter of '76.*
- Use an apostrophe in a contraction to show the omission of letters, for example, *couldn't.*

A. Using the Hyphen and the Apostrophe

On the lines, write the correct form of the boldfaced words including hyphens and apostrophes. If no additional punctuation is needed, write **Correct.**

1. **Wasnt** basketball originally played with a peach basket instead of a net? _____

2. Louisa May Alcott wrote the **bestselling** novel *Little Women.* _____

3. The **worldrenowned** Mexican author Carlos Fuentes published his first book, *Where the Air Is Clear,* in 1958. _____

4. Local journalists are attending an **editors** conference. _____

Hyphens and Apostrophes

More Practice

A. Using the Hyphen and the Apostrophe

In these sentences, underline each word that requires a hyphen and write the corrected word above the underlined word. Then, on the line to the right, write the possessive form of the boldfaced words.

1. Since preChristian times, pirates have roamed the seas, according to **Ramon and Sarah** report.   _____

2. **Achilles** heel was the only spot on his body where he was vulnerable.   _____

3. My greatgrandfather lives a ten **minutes** walk from our home.   _____

4. After **Mr. Elgin** death, his soninlaw was given his bestloved golf clubs.   _____

5. Fully twothirds of the class saw **James** recordbreaking jump.   _____

6. It's **anybody** guess who will be the presidentelect.   _____

7. There were about thirtyfive guests at **Michele and Terry** graduation parties.   _____

8. The preOlympics champion was defeated in the **men** 100meter freestyle.   _____

9. I prefer an Americanstyle breakfast when I visit this **nation** biggest cities.   _____

10. The class is intended to increase the **children** selfreliance.   _____

B. Using the Hyphen and the Apostrophe Correctly

Rewrite each sentence, adding hyphens and apostrophes where necessary.

1. We hadnt seen our exneighbor in three years time before we saw him yesterday.

_____

_____

2. Youll never guess where Luis greatgrandfather spent the winter of 26.

_____

3. Mrs. Whites motherinlaw taught her how to knit Celias and Beths scarves.

_____

4. The lost hikers felt halfdead until they found somebodys abandoned cabin.

_____

For use with Pupil's Edition pp. 265–267

Lesson 6

Hyphens and Apostrophes

Application

A. Proofreading for Correct Punctuation

Underline words that require hyphens or apostrophes in the following paragraph. Then write the correctly punctuated word above each underlined word.

The littleknown story of a pirate named Rachel Wall is one of Bostons bestkept secrets. Rachel was born in 1760 in Carlisle, Pennsylvania. Rachels parents were hardworking farmers, but they werent able to instill their values in Rachel. She left home at a young age and soon married sailor George Wall. In a few years George and Rachel became involved in a scheme with some of Georges friends. Their plan was simple: they made their small fishing ship appear damaged, and Rachel stood alone on the deck waving to passing ships to come to her aid. These wellmeaning crews would enter Rachels trap. After they boarded the now pirate ship, they were attacked and thrown overboard. George and Rachels five man crew would steal their possessions and scuttle their ship. George and Rachels scheme worked for a while, but soon George died in a hurricane. Ironically, Rachel was finally arrested for a crime she claimed she did not commitstealing a womans bonnet on the streets of Boston. On October 7, 1789, Rachel Wall was hanged for assault in Boston Commons.

B. Writing with Correct Punctuation

Follow the directions to write and punctuate sentences correctly.

1. Write a sentence in which one part of a word is carried over from one line to the next.

_____

_____

2. Write a sentence that uses an apostrophe to show possession of a noun ending in *s*.

_____

3. Write a sentence that includes a compound adjective.

_____

4. Write a sentence that spells out a fraction.

_____

5. Write a sentence that discusses joint possession by two people and uses apostrophes appropriately.

_____

_____

CHAPTER 11

Quotation Marks

Reteaching

Use **quotation marks** at the beginning and at the end of a direct quotation. **Do not use** quotation marks to set off an indirect quotation. Punctuate a speaker's words with a comma, question mark, or exclamation point inside quotation marks. Place a comma after explanatory words, such as *he said*, at the beginning of a sentence.

> Denise asked, "Did you hear the thunder?"

Enclose both parts of a divided quotation in **quotation marks.** Do not capitalize the first word of the second part unless it begins a new sentence.

> "I thought I heard it," Steve answered, "but the sound could have been a jet."

In dialogue, begin a new paragraph each time the speaker changes, and use a separate set of **quotation marks.**

Use single **quotation marks** when you write a quotation within a quotation.

> "My little sister always says, 'I'm afraid of the loud noise,' " explained Denise.

Put a colon or a semicolon outside the closing **quotation mark.**

> That storm is what meteorologists call a "Class F3"; it is quite severe.

If a sentence that includes a quotation is a question or an exclamation, place the question mark or exclamation point outside the **quotation marks.**

> Have you ever heard the song "Thunder in the Night"?

Use **quotation marks** to set off or enclose the titles of magazine articles, chapters, short stories, TV episodes, essays, poems, and songs.

Using Quotation Marks

Add quotation marks, commas, and end marks where necessary in each sentence or conversation.

1. How do you know when a tornado is a possibility? Ms. Antine asked her class.

2. Linda answered, The National Weather Service issues an advisory bulletin called a tornado watch.

3. Does the watch bulletin mean, asked Ms. Antine, that a tornado has been sighted?

4. No, said Paul. It only means that conditions are right for the formation of a tornado.

5. Here is what I read in the *World Book Encyclopedia* article about tornadoes: Tornadoes have uprooted large trees, overturned railroad cars, and carried such heavy objects as automobiles hundreds of feet or meters, said Heidi.

6. My science teacher says that tornadoes usually occur in late spring when cool, dry air from the north collides with warm, humid air from the south, offered Bob.

7. I remember in August 1999, a tornado hit downtown Salt Lake City, said Ms. Antine. It hit in late summer in an area that almost never has tornadoes.

8. Can we ever be totally safe from tornadoes? asked Bob. I doubt it.

For use with Pupil's Edition pp. 268–271

Lesson 7

Quotation Marks

More Practice

A. Writing Sentences with Quotation Marks

Add quotation marks, commas, and end marks where necessary in each sentence.
If the sentence is correct, write **Correct** on the line.

1. The whole secret of the study of nature wrote George Sand
   lies in learning how to use one's eyes. _____

2. Zachary asked why no one had given him a surprise party. _____

3. To Build a Fire is the name of a short story by Jack London. _____

4. Don't count your chickens warned Aesop before they are hatched. _____

5. Here's what the ad for the resort says: You'll enjoy first-class treatment
   once you walk through the door Karen said. Let's go there on our vacation! _____

6. When Archimedes discovered the natural law of buoyancy,
   he exclaimed Eureka _____

7. Is your favorite poem called Stopping by Woods on a Snowy Evening _____

8. "That water is moving too fast for swimming," warned Jacob.
   "Well, I'm certainly not going to swim here in that case,"
   answered Ahmed. _____

9. "This piece by Johann Sebastian Bach the critic began reflects the
   energy and optimism of the Baroque Period, with its driving rhythms
   and major chords.
   "On the other hand, this piece by Beethoven highlights the
   emotionalism that was part of the Romantic rebellion. _____

10. The instruction manual says Be sure to unplug the printer
    before opening it read Rebecca. _____

B. Using Quotation Marks in a Dialogue

Add quotation marks, commas, and end marks where necessary.

Listen, do you hear that thunder asked Emilio. I'd better go before the
lightning starts.

Didn't you know that if we can hear thunder, lightning has already struck
asked Tim.

Emilio thought about what Tim had said. Then he asked Tim where he had
gotten his information.

Tim answered I clearly remember that this is what the *World Book
Encyclopedia* says: Scientists know that the sound of thunder is caused by the
violent expansion of air that has been heated by lightning. He added That
means that the lightning has to come first; don't you agree?

In that case said Emilio I'll just stay here until the storm is over.

CHAPTER 11

Quotation Marks

Application

A. Correcting Misuse of Quotation Marks

Rewrite the following sentences, using quotation marks, commas, and end marks correctly.

1. What was that TV episode about storms called"? Mary asked. "Was it Tornado Watch?

   _____

   _____

2. "Was that the one in which the announcer said The winds in tornadoes are the most violent ones on the face of the earth." replied Jason?

   _____

   _____

3. Mary said, I learned about the most destructive tornado in history. It killed 689 people in Missouri and Illinois in 1925"!

   _____

   _____

4. Some people "said Philip" describe the sound of a tornado as "the roar of an oncoming train;" at least, that's what I heard.

   _____

   _____

5. "All I know is if I ever hear that a tornado on is its way Jason said, I'm heading for the basement"!

   _____

   _____

B. Writing with Quotation Marks

Write a dialogue for a short story about two strangers who seek shelter from a rainstorm in the same place. Make sure that you indicate clearly who is speaking. Use quotation marks and other punctuation marks correctly. Use a separate piece of paper if necessary.

   _____

   _____

   _____

   _____

For use with Pupil's Edition pp. 268–271

Lesson 8 · Ellipses and Italics

Reteaching

Use **ellipsis points** (. . .) to indicate the omission of a word, phrase, line, or paragraph within a quoted passage. If the omission comes at the end of a sentence, use an end mark after the **ellipsis points.**

> Bartram and his little son, . . . sat watching the same line-kiln that had been the scene of Ethan Brand's solitary and meditative life. . . .
>
> Nathaniel Hawthorne, "Ethan Brand"

Use **italics,** or **underlining** or **underscoring,** to set off titles of books, newspapers, and magazines. Italicize the titles of plays, movies, television series, epic (long) poems, long musical compositions, and works of art.

Use **italics** to set off words when referred to as words and foreign words or phrases that are not common in English.

> What does the word *persona* mean?

A. Using Italics

Underline the words that should be italicized in each sentence.

1. The epic poem The Divine Comedy by Dante Alighieri gives the author's view of life after death.
2. The TV comedy My Life and Times is doing well with viewers aged 25 to 49.
3. What exactly does the word lexicon mean?
4. Acting has become Judith's raison d'être, or reason for being.
5. The funniest, most heart-warming play I have ever seen is Harvey.

B. Using Ellipses

Read the passage and then compare the numbered quotes below the passage to it. Decide whether ellipses have been used correctly in the quotes. If there are too few or too many ellipsis points, underline the ellipses. If the ellipsis points are used correctly in the quote, write **Correct** on the line.

> The people came out of their houses and smelled the hot stinging air and covered their noses from it. And the children came out of the houses, but they did not run or shout as they would have done after a rain.
>
> John Steinbeck, *The Grapes of Wrath*

1. "The people . . . . smelled the hot stinging air and covered their noses from it. And the children came out of the houses, but they did not run or shout as they would have done after a rain."   _____

2. "The people . . . smelled the hot stinging air and covered their noses from it. And the children came out of the houses, but they did not run or shout as they would have done after a rain."   _____

3. "The people . . . smelled the hot stinging air and covered their noses from it. . . And the children came out of the houses, but they did not run or shout . . ."   _____

Ellipses and Italics

More Practice

A. Using Italics

In each sentence below, underline words that should be italicized but are not. Write
Correct on the line if the sentence is italicized correctly.

1. Fran sneezed, and together we said, "Gesundheit!"   _____

2. Edgar Allan Poe's short story "The Tell-Tale Heart" is a frightening
   look at a mind in pain.   _____

3. The word boom is onomatopoetic, that is, it sounds like what it means.   _____

4. The novel Native Son is required reading at many high schools.   _____

5. The Agatha Christie play The Mousetrap has played in London
   for many years.   _____

6. The word *freedom* has different meanings for different people.   _____

7. When you finish reading your copy of Sports Today, may I borrow it?   _____

8. I found some of my information for the report from the encyclopedia
   article entitled "Dewey Decimal Classification."   _____

B. Using Ellipses

Read the following passage. Then choose the passage below in which ellipsis
points have been used correctly to quote the passage. Circle the number before
the correct passage.

. . . "Love is what is needed," we chant and then sit back, and the world
goes on as before. The fact is we can only love what we know personally. And
we cannot know much. In public affairs, in the rebuilding of civilisation,
something much less dramatic and emotional is needed, namely, tolerance.
Tolerance is a very dull virtue. It is boring. Unlike love, it has always had a bad
press. It is negative. It merely means putting up with people, being able to
stand things. No one has ever written an ode to tolerance or raised a statue to
her. Yet this is the quality which will be most needed after the war. This is the
sound state of mind which we are looking for. This is the only force which will
enable different races and classes and interests to settle down together to the
work of reconstruction.

E. M. Forster, "Tolerance," *Two Cheers for Democracy*

1. . . . "Love is what is needed," we chant and then sit back, and the world goes
   on as before. The fact is we can only love what we know personally. And we
   cannot know much. In public affairs, . . . something much less dramatic and
   emotional is needed, namely tolerance.

2. . . ."Love is what is needed," we chant and then sit back, . . . and the world
   goes on as before. . . .The fact is we can only love what we know personally.
   And we cannot know much. . . . , something much less dramatic and emotional
   is needed, namely, tolerance.

For use with Pupil's Edition pp. 272–273

Lesson 8 # Ellipses and Italics   *Application*

A. Writing with Italics

Complete all these sentences with a title. Underline every word that should
be italicized. Remember to include appropriate end punctuation mark.

1. I think the most worthwhile show on television this year is _____

because _____

2. A book I think everyone should read is _____. I chose it

because _____

3. I think the best poem I ever read is _____ because

_____

4. I think the most memorable play I ever saw is _____

because _____

B. Using Ellipses

You want to quote the following passage from *The Grapes of Wrath* by John
Steinbeck, but you have room for only four lines. Read the passage and decide
which words or phrases you can omit and still maintain the sense of the paragraph.
Rewrite your revised paragraph on the lines below, and on a separate piece of
paper if necessary. Use ellipses to show where you have omitted words.

Outside, a man walking along the edge of the highway crossed over and
approached the truck. He walked slowly to the front of it, put his hand on the
shiny fender, and looked at the *No Riders* sticker on the windshield. For a
moment he was about to walk on down the road, but instead he sat on the
running board on the side away from the restaurant. He was not over thirty.
His eyes were very dark brown and there was a hint of brown pigment in his
eyeballs. His cheek bones were high and wide, and strong deep lines cut
down his cheeks, in curves beside his mouth. His upper lip was long, and
since his teeth protruded, the lips stretched to cover them, for this man kept
his lips closed. His hands were hard, with broad fingers and space between
thumb and forefinger and the hams of his hands were shiny with callus.

_____

_____

_____

_____

CHAPTER 11